Your gift from the LGBTQ+ Real Estate Alliance

A LIMITLESS EXPERIENCE

Danielle,

great to meet you!

Love,

grant Mull

Grant's dramatic life story and his "Top of Heart worldview" that emerged from it align powerfully with Compass' top values – finding your place in the world (our mission), bouncing back from adversity with great passion, and the realization that we can't succeed alone. This book reminds us of what we already know while also giving us a new way of implementing it. *Top of Heart* reminds us that the real keys to success in business are the relationships we nurture. Grant does a great job of combining his fresh business perspectives and gripping personal story into a brand new model, while adding real world urgency that will compel anyone in business to make this book a "must read."

—Robert Reffkin, Founder & CEO, Compass Real Estate

Top of Heart is a work of art. It reads like watching a movie. Grant is as authentic, vulnerable, and real as he wishes us all to be in this life story with lessons powerful enough to save us from ourselves. It is time to quit marketing to strangers and it is time to start communicating with friends. It is time for us to take our insatiable appetite for what we don't have and replace it with an insatiable appreciation for what we do have. Bless Grant for writing *Top of Heart,* because every reader will be blessed by his words.

—Michael J Maher, CEO of REFERCO.com
and bestselling author of *(7L) The Seven Levels of*
Communication* and *Miracle Morning for Real Estate Agents

Who would have thought to write a book that combines memoir, addiction, and a groundbreaking relationship-building model for business? Is that a "normal" business book formula? Probably not, but *Top of Heart* works, in the way an unusual but delicious sandwich does – like Elvis's favorite, peanut butter and banana. It works because to really understand *why* Grant's "Top of Heart" model is so good and so necessary in business today, you need to get on the rollercoaster with him and experience his gripping life story. You need to know how he almost died, how "Top of Heart" was a direct result of his rebirth, and how it can create a rebirth for any of us in the business of building relationships. Am I saying

Elvis would have loved this book? That's for you to decide. In the meantime, I'm already experiencing success by applying Grant's techniques and exercises to build more meaningful relationships with my clients and prospects!

—Alexander Watkins, Founder, Eat My Words and author of *Hello, My Name Is Awesome*

Top of Heart takes you on a messy introspection of the twists, tribulations, and disasters life serves... and then shows you how finding motivation and purpose enables you to change your world for the better. Heart-rending read. Inspiring story.

—Stefan Swanepoel, *New York Times* **and** *Wall Street Journal* **bestselling author**

As someone who has experienced traumatic events in life and found a way to move forward from personal challenges, I have great admiration for how Grant has done the same *and*, on top of that, how he has taken those lessons and integrated them into his "Top of Heart" business model. The more I read and absorbed Grant's explanation of his "Top of Heart worldview," where relationships rule and drive transactions (versus the opposite), the more flashing light bulbs went off in my head, like – YES, THIS! Not to sound cliché, but this book is a "must read" for everyone in business and certainly for my real estate colleagues.

—Maya Vander, real estate advisor, cast member of Netflix series *Selling Sunset*

Open. Honest. Torment transforming into triumph. If you prefer reading stories of people whose personal struggles have been minimal, have been great at what they do, and now want to show you how you too can be great... this is not the book for you. But if you want to read a captivating memoir about a man who struggled with who he was and his personal addictions, then overcame those circumstances, and uses that story to teach one of the most powerful business and sales lessons anyone will ever learn... then this is the book for you! The writing will grab you. The story will touch you. And the lessons will change you. *Top of Heart* by Grant Muller is a great book and I encourage every entrepreneur, salesperson, or business leader to read it!

—Jeff C. West, award-winning author of *The Unexpected Tour Guide* and bestselling co-author of *Said the Lady with the Blue Hair: 7 Rules for Success in Direct Sales Wrapped in a Wonderful Lesson for Life.*

By courageously and candidly sharing his story, without holding back or censoring himself, Grant has chosen to be more than an author, more than a business thought leader – he has chosen to be an advocate.

—Ryan Hampton, addiction recovery advocate and bestselling author of *American Fix* and *Unsettled*

I've been selling and team building with Avon for over 40 years. I've also side hustled and built teams in other sales organizations, but I am most known for my position in the top five teams in Avon for over two decades. My team numbers in the thousands and are spread across every state in the United States. In direct sales, genuine relationships are key. The relationships with customers and the relationships with team members. Reading Grant's life-changing book *Top of Heart* reinforces and expands upon what I've been teaching and modeling for years. The book not only tells Grant's story of triumph over his addictions and circumstances, but also gives a valuable framework and comprehensive structure to help us grow our numbers while being our most authentic selves along the way. My hope is that every direct seller – and every business owner! – will get Grant's book and use it to grow their business. What a difference it would make for so many!

Lisa M. Wilber, Avon Platinum Executive Leader, award-winning co-author of *Said the Lady with the Blue Hair: 7 Rules for Success in Direct Sales Wrapped in a Wonderful Lesson for Life*

Like many of us, Grant Muller made some very poor choices in life. *Top of Heart* is his bare and compelling life story, revealing both his ups and downs, and the lessons he learned along the way.

—Randy Gage, author of *Radical Rebirth*

TOP OF HEART

HOW A NEW APPROACH TO BUSINESS SAVED MY LIFE, AND COULD SAVE YOURS TOO

GRANT MULLER

First published in Great Britain by Practical Inspiration Publishing, 2023

The moral rights of the author have been asserted

Top of Heart® is a registered trademark of Grant Muller LLC

ISBN   9781788604369 (paperback)
       9781788605090 (hardback)
       9781788604383 (epub)
       9781788604376 (mobi)

Please note: The author's intention to remain true to the story means that this book contains street language and references to drug use. In order to preserve the privacy of certain individuals, some names and stories have been altered.

Every effort has been made to trace copyright holders and to obtain their permission for the use of copyright material. The publisher apologizes for any errors or omissions and would be grateful if notified of any corrections that should be incorporated in future reprints or editions of this book.

Want to bulk-buy copies of this book for your team and colleagues? We can introduce case studies, customize the content, and co-brand *Top of Heart* to suit your business's needs.

Please email info@practicalinspiration.com for more details.

Practical Inspiration
Publishing

For the loves of my life: Adrian, Winston, Paddington.

To Mom, Dad, Candice, Mark: Thank you for never giving up.

*To Dave: Thank you for teaching me and showing me
what recovery looks like.*

*And for each and every person (and program) that has believed in me and
helped to save my life in one form or another: I could never pay it all back,
but I will spend the rest of my life trying.*

CONTENTS

FOREWORD

Imagine yourself at the movies: completely captivated, riveted by the story of a person who is on such a downward spiral, most likely heading toward certain death, that you simply cannot take your eyes off the screen. While you sense the protagonist will eventually be okay (after all, it is just a movie), the screenwriters have painted a picture of such despair, such hopelessness and desperation, that you can't imagine how they'll possibly pull it off.

You're about to watch that movie. You're holding it in your hands right now.

Only in this case, the story is true. In just a moment, you're going to begin a wild ride with the author that will forever reshape the way you view life and business.

First, though...

I had the honor of meeting the "movie's" protagonist, Grant Muller, in January 2018 at one of Kathy Tagenel's and my Go-Giver Academy events where he was part of a deliberately intimate group of top sales professionals. We spent two days together digging deep into each others' businesses – strategizing, problem-solving, and collaborating.

Grant was an engaged and dynamic participant, a true leader, adding much more to the two days than he could have possibly received. We would soon come to realize; this is Grant's essence. The man is a giver, and the success of his business comes from his ability to quickly connect with others on a deeply genuine heart-to-heart level and provide value like few others.

As impressed as Kathy and I were with Grant, and as much as we liked him right from the start, it would be another year before we would have the privilege of *really* getting to know him, and his story – the "behind the scenes" of his remarkable success.

As you are about to see for yourself, he has been through hell and back, and through it again.

Fortunately, he came back again that final time. The world is a much, much better place because he did so. It's a much better place because he is in it.

Success stories have a palpable energy, especially ones featuring protagonists who rise out of the ashes like the proverbial phoenix. These stories are my favorites because they inspire, encourage, delight, and show us what is *truly* possible!

And sometimes they take all your (my, our) excuses away. This is when you see what a person did to lift themselves from the rock bottom of raw existence, barely alive, avoiding death by wits alone (and perhaps some luck), and eventually arriving where most people can only dream of being.

This is Grant's story. It's the story of a talented, entrepreneurial, intelligent human being whom you would trust with your business and with your life.

It is also the story of an addict.

He is a recovering one (15 years at the time of writing), but an addict just the same – which goes to show the true power of Grant's remarkable "Top of Heart" message at the center of the book. He is living proof that in order to connect and bond with someone on a deep level, to nurture a real relationship, you first need to do the work to find out who they are as a person. You need to go behind the scenes and discover their life story.

You are about to learn Grant's life story, and then you will be able to take those lessons and apply them to learning *other* people's life stories. As a business professional, this will change the way you operate at work and in life.

This generosity of spirit and sharing everything he has lived and everything he knows, in service of others, is why Grant is the very embodiment of what we refer to as a "Go-Giver." Everything about Grant's "Top of Heart" message is congruent with that philosophy.

The "Top of Heart" model will walk you through what it takes to have a successful business, one based on creating relationships of mutual giving and caring, and one in which you genuinely want those whose lives you touch to be better off for it. Regardless of whether you sell real estate or are involved in any other type of enterprise, the business-building principles that Grant shares in the latter part of the book will help lift you to great heights – if you apply them.

This absolutely fascinating book is one movie featuring two journeys – a personal one and a business one. But together those journeys create one life, and they reveal the entire essence of Grant Muller.

And if you're like me you'll be gripped from the very first page, unable to put the book down! You will marvel at how low a person can sink, and then how high they can rise.

And you will be infinitely better off for having read it.

Wishing you Stratospheric Success!

Bob Burg, co-author of *The Go-Giver*

PROLOGUE

August, 2007

The big rig horn jolted me from my gentle sleep. My steering wheel was resting between my legs and my right foot was (luckily) riding the brake pedal. I was swerving between four lanes, picking up speed... 50, 60, 70 mph. I had been steering with my legs in my sleep. Sort of. I was exiting the Western side of Eisenhower tunnel (a 1.7-mile tunnel under the continental divide in Colorado, 11,000 ft above sea level), and my exit was going to be permanent if I couldn't find a way to slow down.

The tunnel ends with a long, steep descent down a treacherous Colorado highway. There was a row of traffic four lanes wide following me as I had slowed and weaved in the tunnel. Impatient drivers in cars and trucks were blaring horns, but they were too scared to pass me as my pace quickened with the hill. My first thought was that I was getting pulled over by cops, but when I looked I was relieved to see only civilians in my rear-view mirror.

My second and equally irrational thought was that I was being followed by a very large contingent of undercover agents. After all, you're not paranoid if they really ARE following you. Third, I remembered the crystal meth on board and my urgent mission

– deliver meth to the mountain town where they happily pay a premium for the stuff. *Oh, the stuff.*

Before I had solved my problem of steering an out-of-control car down a very steep hill, my attention turned back to the stuff. How do I get to the stuff in its hiding place so I can refuel? If I just dip in and steal a little, the buyers won't notice. I had long ago made a pact with myself – I would never cut the dope. This wasn't an ethical stand; it was a practical one. I lived both on it and for it and couldn't stand to dilute its impact. After all, I survived on my own inventory. Instead, I had devised a different solution – a buying scale and a selling scale, each calibrated for my benefit. I had the selling scale with me. It was set to make less than a gram look like a gram, giving me room to breathe… it in.

I woke up. Again. Damn – must have blacked out. Coming back to life was always disappointing. The cars were no longer lined up behind me, and somehow I had straightened my path down the mountain. Straight down the mountain highway, clocking closer to 90 now, my foot no longer resting on the brake pedal.

It's hard to explain what it feels like to wake up behind the wheel of a car careening down a steep mountain path. It's hard to explain the feeling because I had no feeling. I wasn't scared about the mountain, or the out-of-control car, or impending death. I was scared about not getting to the dope. I was scared I wouldn't get the chance to take one more hit before I went flying off the side of the mountain.

I had been up for a week or so at this point with no sleep at all, except for the little catnap I had just enjoyed. While a week is a long-ish time to be awake, it isn't close to the longest time for me. But it was enough to reach that place where you are in a permanent dream state. You disconnect from yourself and everything around you. Except the dope – you never disconnect from that. I was post verbal, post intellect, and in a spot where I knew only one language: D-O-P-E.

I used the momentum of the speed I had banked to cross three lanes of traffic in an instant and take the very next exit. I checked the rear view again for flashing lights. Surely a string of 911 calls had bombarded a small-town switchboard with word of vehicular lunacy. Off the highway now, I pulled to the side of the road and shoved the car into park. I got to the stash of dope fast and ate it. *No time for a pipe. Tastes like drain cleaner mixed with Sudafed. Just a little. That didn't do it, maybe a bit more. Ooh, there it is… I bet a bit more will help or maybe… Ah yes, the back of my head is tingling, my heart is exploding, and my vision is vibrating. All is well again.*

Revived at last, I snapped to attention and remembered my mission. Getting back on the highway, once again invincible, I had absolutely no concern about the Highway Patrol. The combination of meth and sleeplessness meant I switched swiftly back and forth between fearlessness and paranoia. Fearless now, superhero powers intact, I made it to the predetermined, secluded parking lot and killed the engine. It was dark and quiet. I could hear my heart screaming in my head – boom-boom-boom-boom-boom in very quick succession.

In the stillness, I imagined how the next 30 minutes might go. Was I about to get arrested for selling drugs to undercover agents? Was I going to get shot in the head and robbed for the drugs? Either was likely.

But those risks didn't matter to me because I didn't own the drugs I was selling. THAT was the risk that mattered. They were bought on credit, and my creditor wouldn't sue me if I failed to pay him. He had more violent methods to enforce his contractual rights. This wasn't theoretical knowledge – I had seen his brutal methods up close. Even worse than suffering his special brand of punishment would be banishment from the crystal meth, my one and only love.

In the end, the buyers showed up and happily paid me the agreed upon price… for the actual weight, not the promised weight. Savvy. Damnit. Everyone knows a nickel can be used to easily calibrate a scale when on the go – a nickel weighs exactly 5 grams. They brought a goddamn nickel.

On my way back down the mountain, I didn't have enough money for the debt (much less, in fact, because I took more out of the bag at the last minute and smoked it while waiting for the buyers to show up) and I had barely enough dope to fuel the drive back to Denver. And when I didn't return with payment, I'd have to go on the run from the guy on the run – a "top ten most wanted" Colorado fugitive wanted by just about every law enforcement agency in the state.

He's going to kill me.

INTRODUCTION

June, 2010

About 40 minutes into my 45-minute breakfast meeting, I realized I might have a problem. My second meeting had just arrived early, and I could see her announcing her arrival at the host stand.

My current breakfast date showed up late, going on and on about traffic and weather and construction and every other conceivable excuse for his tardiness. He spent hours and hours (at least it felt like it) pouring over the menu as if it were the first menu he had ever encountered, and when he couldn't decide, he ordered the pancake platter AND the scrambled eggs and potatoes.

Before the server had finished writing our orders, he launched into a non-stop tour of every potential topic of conversation. There were bits and pieces from every corner of his life. It was like a tour of Europe with just five minutes in each country. Frankly, none of the countries interested me. None of the countries were about me. This was supposed to be my opportunity to impress, to network, to build relationships, and to further my real estate career. I couldn't get a word in, and my next breakfast date was scheduled to start in just five minutes. Tick tock.

After hustling online lead-generation programs for years, I had seen the light. "Real estate is a relationship business," they told me. My coaches advised me to get face to face with people – LOTS of people! – and build rapport. I was on a mission to do just that. I had a special tracker, and I was required to keep careful score of each of these interactions, a check mark for each person.

I had embarked on this new relationships program with a fresh excitement, but I was learning quickly that it's tough to shove this many people into one calendar. I was required to see immense numbers of prospects face to face every week. I was rushing from meeting to meeting, sometimes running to and from my car as if I was on a hectic scavenger hunt. The people blurred together until they weren't people any more, just tracker fodder.

Then, I read about an idea to hold several meetings, one after another, at the same place to reduce my travel time. Brilliant. This breakfast meeting was my first attempt to execute the new strategy. I would stay put and let the targets come to me, one after the other. How many prospects I would be able to check off in my tracker with this efficient plan of attack! The manic rush for numbers had blurred my relationship-building vision.

The waitress had returned, obviously wanting to turn the table. My lap was filled with a pile of shredded napkins from the stress of trying to shut this guy up and put an end to his selfish sales pitch (this was supposed to be about ME!), and I was making apologetic eyes at my second breakfast date as she glared at me from the busy restaurant's standing-room-only waiting area. I was mortified.

Finally, after watching this guy ignore all my most blatant social cues, I got the nerve to interrupt breakfast meeting number one to explain that I had another meeting waiting. In one motion, he stood up abruptly, dropped $10 on the table for his $40 breakfast, chugged the remainder of his cappuccino, and shoved his sticky syrup hand in mine for an awkward syrup-meets-grape-jelly handshake. He was off. As I watched him crab-walk between the tightly woven tables, I knew I didn't want to see him again and

I knew I would. Sales is a numbers game, and the tracker would need to be filled again next month.

Breakfast date number two approached my table immediately, annoyed and rightly so. Here she was finally, a well-regarded and well-connected, up-and-coming attorney. I had been looking forward to our meeting for some time. She had spoken at a recent event, and I was moved by her community leadership and brilliant perspective. She clearly cared deeply about making a real difference for people. I looked forward to an engaging conversation and perhaps making a new networking connection. I was mostly hoping that all her rich attorney friends could become my rich attorney clients.

I wanted to impress her and, instead, she was sitting across from me with someone else's half- eaten eggs, pancakes, and used silverware staring back at her. Gross. Tracker score = 2. New relationship score = 0. Later, I found out that breakfast date number one, who had been referred to me, had the nerve to say that he felt like "just a number" in my networking game. The gall. What about breakfast date number two? Let's just say she wasn't scrambling for a repeat of someone else's cold eggs.

Heart-based business

It's been quite a journey for me from homelessness to $1.2 million in sales commission last year. I will never forget the first time that number danced on my laptop screen. I looked over my shoulder and then back again at the screen. "You wanna dance with ME?!"

I love this party and you're invited. Ditch the cheap cologne and tacky pick-up lines. Hunting and tracking "prospects" or "leads" or "targets" before dumping them into a "funnel" is no longer serving anyone.

That early attempt at building a business based on relationships was a colossal failure, but it held key lessons. As a real estate agent for about 14 years now, my drive to succeed has led me down just about every conceivable path toward real estate enlightenment.

It's been a long and expensive tour through many different sales, lead-generation, marketing, and coaching programs. I've learned a lot and share the credit for my success with many cherished teachers. The strategies I learned from them helped me move out of the storage unit I was living in at the beginning of my real estate career and into my own home. Somehow, though, there was always something missing. I couldn't quite break free of the sales roller coaster. There would be a good month or two and then right back to barely paying the bills.

Making my way from the meth nightmare on the mountain highway to the breakfast meeting was a long journey. On the way to saving my life, I learned to get real for the first time. While stumbling into my own humanity, I uncovered the distinction that unlocked the world for me.

If you're an entrepreneur, a small business owner, a leader, or a salesperson, you are likely getting hammered with calls and emails and online promotions, all promising to lead you to a magical land of golden leads and platinum appointments. Instead of selling more, we buy more – of other people's stuff. The balance is broken.

Some individuals in business, particularly in industries that seem to be set in their ways (such as real estate), might not be aware of this. They slog away, on the grind, to hit sales metrics. They choke down sales tactics to win games that, for most of them, are counter to their very nature. They put on their sales hat and suddenly their humanity slips away. They put on their sales hat and suddenly their empathy slips away. They put on their sales hat and, bit by bit, they adopt a completely different personality.

I lost myself just like that and suffered a near-death disconnection between my head, my hands, and my heart. As you're about to find out, it didn't just destroy me professionally, it almost killed me off completely.

Whether you are facing a life-threatening addiction or a lackluster, unfulfilling sales career, I'll introduce you to the Top-of-Heart worldview that I discovered as I went to war with my own struggles. But this isn't just my story, it's yours too. This book aims to help you achieve more without the endless hustle of manipulative sales tactics and scripts that don't quite feel authentic (not even close). I've got news for you – no matter how much you achieve, it won't bring you true fulfillment. Achievement comes from fulfillment, not the other way around.

Getting real saved my life and you're about to see how. My comeback required all of me – head, hands, and heart. By the end of this book, you'll have a clear picture of the mindset, skillset, and heartset to get EXACTLY what you want in business and in life.

PART ONE: ME

CHAPTER 1.

WHERE HAVE ALL THE

COWBOYS GONE?

When you're a kid on your way up in South Africa, you believe that all of America is like *Bonanza*. There must be cowboys everywhere in their huge hats and heeled boots. And horses! Cowboys have horses, lots and lots of horses. I have been obsessed with horses since a preschool encounter with a grocery store coin-operated kiddie ride. From that moment on, I was dead set on the real thing and my folks heard about little else.

Born in South Africa in the early '70s, my first seven years were pleasant enough. We had Christmas on the (all-white) beach every year and enjoyed close friendships with our (all-white) neighbors after (all-white) school. It was much like I imagine it must have been growing up in the US in the '50s – a segregated world. Even the one TV station was black and white. I recognize now we had been served huge, oversized scoops of vanilla ice cream privilege.

At seven, I got word that we were moving to the land of cowboys. I was sad to leave my friends behind, but my excitement about becoming a cowboy swiftly overcame any sense of loss.

My very own herd of horses are waiting! The air-time from South Africa to the US was arduous, but the first leg, which was my first flight ever, was just a two-hour hop from Cape Town to Johannesburg. We settled into the smoky 737 (it was the '70s, after all) as a happy family of five, and, like so many immigrants before and after us, we were off to the land where cowboy dreams can come true for everyone.

We were seated above the wings and the wheels. The scenery was enchanting, and I was sure the clouds would be even more billowy as we got closer to America. *I bet America has the BEST clouds!*

More than halfway through the flight, the pilot shoved his office door open and strode toward us, scowling, with a mystery mission all his own. Stopping right next to our seats and crouching in the aisle, I began wondering if my dad had my ticket to prove that I belonged on the plane. My seven-year-old imagination was busily writing a compelling news headline – "Family of five discovered with a boy that doesn't belong and asked to exit the plane mid-flight." I didn't understand why yet, but I knew that, somehow, I didn't belong.

Instead, the pilot ignored us and began to pull up the carpet in the aisle. My little boy instincts knew he wasn't happy as he tugged and fought with the carpet tiles, muttering something under his breath. Another pilot made an appearance at one point and the flight attendants huddled nearby, watching anxiously. The pilots were whispering to each other and they seemed agitated.

Who is flying our plane?! They were detaching the actual floor now. One pilot remained, lying fully flat in the aisle and peering through a big hole where the carpet used to be. *Can he see the ground?!* He smelled like an important grown-up, kind of sweaty with heavy aftershave undertones. His wingman returned to the office to make a calm and polite announcement about our impending death.

Over the intercom, his voice squeaked the three most terrifying words an airline captain can utter: "Please remain calm." The good news? Just two sets of tires had burst during takeoff. The bad news? A 737 only has three sets of tires. We spent the next two hours circling the airport while burning fuel and learning how to position ourselves for the imminent emergency landing.

Head between knees. Everyone on the plane was frightened, except Dad. He knew it was going to be okay. I wasn't sure how he knew, but he knew. It was a big relief, and I wished that all the nervous passengers were lucky enough to have a dad like mine who had the inside scoop and the mindset to go with it.

Plunging toward Earth, I thought about the horses that were waiting for me in America. Would they meet me in heaven? Can everyone else hear my heart pounding? The impact itself was somewhat anticlimactic. Later, my dad told me he had ignored the head-between-knees instructions and watched our landing out the window. I didn't tell him that I also ignored the instructions and watched him watch our landing out the window. Sparks flew as the two naked wheels touched down first. Rubber exploded as the front wheel eventually made contact much too fast. The fire engines lining the foam-filled runway prepared for the worst. We were offloaded directly onto the tarmac and into waiting buses. Several relatively mundane plane rides later, we arrived in Denver, Colorado.

Mile high

There were no horses in sight, just plenty of snow. *Where are all the cowboys?* I had never seen snow and that was fun. I played with it until my hands prickled with white hot pain. "That is only going to make it worse," my aunt warned as I turned on the warm water and shoved my frozen little fingers in the sink, desperate for relief. Oh boy, was she right!

We had arrived midway through the school year and I was sentenced to the second grade in a private Catholic school in mid-January. The alien boy from South Africa was about to brave the mile-high winterscape to somehow fit into a social hierarchy established years before in kindergarten.

Jungle boy

When you're a kid on your way up in the US, you believe all of Africa is like *The Jungle Book*. I was a funny talker from a funny land. I had no clue about popular phenomena of the day such as *Star Wars* and *Sesame Street*. In the second grade, different is not cool; it's a stain.

Welcome, jungle boy, to a strange land of kickball (*what the heck is THIS game?*) and foreign Catholic rituals. We weren't Catholic, but the public schools were lacking. The nuns were mean and called me "weird," a new word to me. Judging by the contempt with which it was uttered, this uniquely American insult landed right where it was aimed. The teachers levied punishment with rulers to knuckles – much kinder than the bare-bottom canings in front of class that I had experienced for "talking too much" in South Africa.

Recess was hell. It was clear that I didn't belong. Wandering from one little group of boys to the next, each group closed ranks as I approached. Staring at the back of heads, the snickering stung. *Why am I being punished?* Eventually abandoning interest in, or hope of, joining the boys in their games, I made my way to the girls with their long plastic jump ropes.

I taught the girls a new game I made up on the spot. "I'll be the cowboy and you be the horsey. These plastic jump ropes run through your mouth and into my hands. They are my reins. GIDDY UP!" Over the next few weeks, parents panicked as their daughters developed horrible sores in the corners of their mouths. It seemed some mystery sickness was plaguing these sweet innocents. Or worse.

Imaginary shame was leveraged, and the girls protected our dark little secret as girls are too often taught to do. The game was ruined, though, and I was sent back to the boy's side, left to count the minutes until recess was over. The mean nuns were a welcome reprieve from the meaner second-grade boys.

My differences were clear to all the boys long before they were even a hint to me. It wasn't just my foreign accent and my foreign clothes. There was something else. It was a total lack of interest in their sportsball and their dinosaur toys and their boyish roughhousing. "You belong with the girls," they said. They were cruel and I retreated.

One tenuous friendship developed, but he turned on me when the others discovered his treachery. The boys bullied me mercilessly and then I tested positive, along with the girls, during a cooties outbreak. I was swiftly banished, sent to even further outposts on the playground. This was merely childhood playground pecking order play, and yet this was not child's play. The bullying was just beginning, and the trauma would have the far-reaching impact that trauma always does.

With no friends from school, I developed a new buddy that lived at the fancy end of our neighborhood in a massive Tudor house. He was a retiree in his seventies with seven (SEVEN?!) cars and a stamp collection that he shared with me. He had three gigantic German shepherds and we played fetch with them for hours and hours. Marveling over his car collection one day, I stumbled across thousands of oval STP stickers in his garage. He let me have one and I took it to school the next day, affixed to my lunchbox.

The sticker drew attention, the first POSITIVE attention I had experienced at school. It seemed that every boy and most of the girls were clamoring to learn where they could get a sticker. It was my first hint of power. Suddenly, I had what they all wanted.

My first business enterprise was born. I procured my friend's entire inventory of STP stickers at no cost and I was in business. I quickly learned my first lesson about sales: Great sales success comes more easily from following and filling demand than creating it. 1 cent. 2 cents. 3 cents. A nickel. Prices soared and it seemed that, no matter how many stickers I brought to school, they were all gone by the end of recess. I loved holding what others wanted. It drew the kids closer to me. Suddenly, I existed and I mattered. They were nicer to me. The money didn't matter much – I was wanted. I belonged.

Much like the mouth sores, sticker shock spread throughout homes all over Denver. It turns out that STP stickers are VERY sticky. Once applied, they do not come off. Ever. STP stickers littered furniture and bikes and houses everywhere. Kids were getting in trouble at home and taking it out on me at school. My supply and my short-lived popularity bottomed out just as the sticker scandal reached its peak. You can buy one of those stickers on eBay today for $5. An investment with me then would have yielded a 9,900% return.

We moved to the suburbs after two years and I was paroled to the wondrous freedom of year-round suburban secular school, with nine weeks of class followed by three weeks of vacation. In fourth grade, I made a best friend, my first best friend ever. It was us against the world as we created an intricate world as detective crime solvers. Suddenly recess was too short and the fun continued after school. It was great to finally have a friend, but I'm sure he noticed I enjoyed hanging out with his mom almost as much as with him. I was clearly different, but he didn't seem to hold it against me.

Unfortunately, my friend was very involved with sports, and this meant I found my way onto a baseball diamond and basketball court. I hadn't grown up with T-ball practice or playing catch with Dad like everyone else, and I simply couldn't understand how or why another little boy would throw a ball so hard at me. They called it "pitching," but I was traumatized a little more with each "pitch." Ducking seemed better than any alternative. Needless to say, I was not a baseball great. To this day, ducking is my instant reaction any time I see something sailing through the air in my direction.

Basketball was a little less hopeless. I was taller than my teammates, and this advantage seemed to make up for my weak ball-handling skills. At our first game, it seemed I had finally found my path to stardom. The crowd cheered louder than I had ever heard as I broke away with the ball and dribbled to the other end. The other boys must have given up because they weren't chasing me. Instead, they all just stood and cheered loudly! My layup maneuver brought the ball home, scoring my first point. I had landed funny and sprained my ankle in the process, but it was worth it for the glory.

And then I found out I had scored for the other team. It turned out they were yelling "wrong way" not "yay." Sitting on the sidelines with ice on my ankle, humiliated, it suddenly dawned on me that figure skating was not going to happen as planned that afternoon. And that was devastating. Dancing on the ice alone somehow made me feel like I belonged. I'm pretty sure I was the only little boy at the game worried about figure skating.

Several years later, at about 12 years old, I finally found my sport.

Friends that lived on a ranch in the country had recently let me ride their horses after I helped them with their chores. This quickly reignited my preschool obsession with horses and, ultimately, my riding dreams.

At the edge of town just past the mall, there were remnants of horse and farm land not yet snatched up by developers. Out of curiosity one day, I left my friends at the mall and took a quarter mile walk in search of horses. Sure enough, there were horses in the barns I had spotted. I quickly tracked down the owners.

"If I clean stalls for you, will you give me riding lessons?"

There was a fast "Yes," and I had my first lesson a few days later. Apparently I was a natural and I felt right at home in the English saddle. My destiny was on horseback and I was right where I belonged.

CHAPTER 2.
IN THE MIDDLE

As we matriculated to middle school, I lost my best friend to football and jock friends and chasing girls. One morning, I met a new boy in choir class and he was unique. Devious. Mysterious. Dan was filled with fascinating stories about his fascinating dad and I was hooked. We would take turns to sneak out to the restroom to "snuff" tobacco. The snuff itself had very little impact. I didn't really understand the point, but my heart virtually exploded with nicotine and adrenaline as I consciously broke rules for the first time in my life. The dizzying thrill of rebellion brought me to life.

Soon, we were hanging out together constantly and cigarettes replaced the snuff. I felt so classy and grown up as I learned to inhale for the first time. Yves Saint Laurent had put their branding on menthol cigarettes and Dan had procured an entire pack. We regularly hung out at a nearby new home development, using partially completed vacant homes as our clubhouse for smoking away the after-school hours and plotting our next nefarious adventures.

Bored one afternoon, Dan and I toured some of the model homes in the development. They had staged the models beautifully and created a lovely picture for homeowners to envision a highly desirable lifestyle. This lifestyle included wine, apparently, and each model had a wine bottle on the dining room table, accompanied by glasses to complete the picture. *Are these really bottles of wine just sitting here? Can we get away with taking these?* We swiped each and every bottle from the model homes that day and, from my first sip of wine, I knew I was home.

I was one with the world. I was cool. I was okay. I was sure. Accepted. Loved. Everything in the universe fell into place. The warmth of the wine going down was my salvation. The tingle in my head joined a tingle somewhere more private. The alcohol and Dan were somehow working together to carry me higher. The combination made me dizzy in ways I wasn't ready to understand. But I knew I liked it and I wanted M-O-R-E.

Over the coming days, we returned to our clubhouse stash of wine and quickly finished off the remaining bottles. When we went back to the model homes to replenish our supply, we were excited to see that the bottles had been thoughtfully replaced, and we helped ourselves again.

A week later, we went "wine shopping" once more. This time, we found the bottles GLUED to the tables. With the least bit of concern, we simply tore the bottles from the tables, bringing some of the table material with us. Our last trip to the model homes confirmed what we had feared – no wine, glued or otherwise. They were on to us. My folks didn't keep a liquor cabinet, so we quickly moved on to Dan's dad's collection. His dad drank the hard stuff and I loved it even more. It seemed like there was never enough. Dan always seemed to know when to stop drinking, but I didn't. I couldn't.

From the very beginning, I had a desperate need to finish it all. It was a sense of urgency, a compulsion, a longing. As inhibitions lifted from the first drink, my feelings for this Dan boy would float through the back of my mind. Before the thoughts could take form, it was a race to erase. If I drank hard and fast, I could stay ahead of the shameful truth. As we moved into the ninth grade, this drive to drink only accelerated.

Higher

To fund my teenage cocktails, I procured a bottle of vodka via a homeless man for a $20 "tip." I divided the bottle into shots, filling little black and gray Kodak film canisters. I diluted the liquor with water to make it go further and sold these shots at a massive markup. As with the STP stickers, I learned that sales is easy when demand is strong. Unlike the STP stickers, I was an enthusiastic fan of this merchandise and I could barely keep up with the demand. My demand.

If it hadn't been for theater and horses, I would not have survived high school. I continued riding in these years and became more and more serious about a career as a horse trainer. In theater, I found something else I was fairly decent at. I loved the acting and the drama of it all. I made friends with kindred spirits, finally fitting in just a bit. I loved escaping into a character and out of my own. I loved being anyone but me. Theater and drinking kept me hidden from myself.

I would take long walks with my girlfriend, Jenny, smoking long menthol cigarettes and talking about our future together. I couldn't picture it like she could, but I was in awe of her. She was pretty and talented and cool, and she was the most adult teenager I had ever met.

Sometimes, we stopped in to chat with our pal Randy, who was a hairdresser in a nearby strip mall. I don't remember how we had gotten to know him, but we would stop in every so often and he would touch up my hair. He seemed to take an interest in us that we appreciated. He treated us like adults. I don't think the word "gay" ever crossed my mind, but I knew he was different. I felt sorry for him because I knew living that lifestyle, whatever that entails, must be hard and lonely.

During the summer between ninth and tenth grade, I stopped in to see Randy once, without Jenny, and he gave me a cut to look my best for a party that night. With just the two of us in the salon, he talked about gay stuff – mostly people he knew, and his boyfriend, and their gay foster kid.

My stomach did backflips. My brain left orbit. I walked out of that salon dazed. I didn't know why. On the way to the party that night, I had a deep sense of foreboding. A storm was coming. A big dark shameful tornado was about to swallow me whole. I didn't know what and I didn't know why, but it was coming. I took long pulls from the Southern Comfort bottle on the passenger seat. *Ah, better. So sweet. So warm. More will be better.* By the time I got to the party, I couldn't even walk inside. I opened the car door and tumbled out and into the space between the car and the sidewalk. I spent the entire night passed out in that gutter.

The next day, I decimated a friend's dad's liquor cabinet. Drunk again, cruising in her car with her, I suggested we stop in to see Randy, who was alone in the salon. He admonished me for my condition and told me to stop running. We didn't know what he meant. *Old people are always saying weird shit.* We sat and talked and joked and hung out for a bit and, when it was time for his next appointment, we got up to leave. I followed my friend out of the salon and he followed us. As I was about to close the salon door and my friend was already getting into her car, Randy said, "Grant, think about WHO you think about."

In that one instant, the wall of denial fell. In that one instant, I knew that Dan had been much more than just a friend to me. He was my first true crush. In that one instant, I knew why I couldn't picture a future with Jenny like she could. In that one instant, I discovered a huge secret about myself that even I hadn't been privy to. My life was over. Any hope of happiness was lost. Now I truly knew why I didn't belong and why I never would.

The pain and trauma from the childhood bullying resurfaced. I had since learned how to mold myself into someone acceptable, or at least passable enough to avoid ridicule. Now I was facing a lifetime of the worst kind of ridicule and very likely an early death in an AIDS ward. This was 1988 – gay was not okay. It wasn't even legal. Identifying myself as a member of this loathed group of people was terrifying. I wasn't just different, I was subhuman.

Over the next couple of years, my worst fears about the worldview of gay folk were realized. I was, after all, living in "the hate state," which was about to pass Amendment 2 expressly prohibiting antidiscrimination protections for gays, lesbians, and bisexuals. Luckily, my family, my theater community, and many in the horse world were much more accepting. As a result, I immersed myself in theater and riding. So much so that I spent the last semester of my senior year in an Executive Internship Program gaining real-world experience as an assistant horse trainer. As that program closed, I was offered a once-in-a-lifetime opportunity to head to Canada and train under a famous Olympic silver medal rider. *ESCAPE.*

CHAPTER 3.
CHURN AND BURN

The day after high school graduation, Dolly Parton boarded a bus and headed to Nashville to chase her country-music-star dreams. Long before "What would Dolly do?" became a t-shirt, I was inspired and ready to act on her inspiration.

On the road from Denver to Toronto, I imagined myself as another superstar, right out of high school and traveling in pursuit of my own dreams. My 18-year-old no-limits mindset was fully intact. Or it was hubris. My new home would be a horse farm where I would ride top-level, international horses. *This is my big break.*

When Dolly landed in Nashville, she found herself lonely and homesick. In this regard, I was no different. And that's where the similarities end. Dolly quickly found fame and superstardom. My path lacked such glamour. And such success.

Instead of riding top-level horses as I had planned, the only time I got close to them was while feeding them or mucking their stalls. I wasn't even grooming horses. It was January in horse country in a small rural town about an hour out of Toronto. I lived in a dusty apartment above the horses with the barn manager couple, who reeked of manure and squandered potential. The horses had superior living arrangements. I didn't go outdoors for the first two months. The only activities at the end of the grueling workday were eating and passing out, utterly exhausted. It was all icicles and frozen rural Canadian countryside anyway.

After a few weeks of feeding the animals, mucking stalls, and sweeping for 12 hours a day, I was gradually given more responsibility, first to groom the horses and eventually to ride them. Mostly I rode the problem horses, and my riding improved dramatically under the watchful eye of my trainer, a former Olympian. We had Olympic gold medal guests too. The equestrian community is tightly knit (and tightly wound, but that's another book) and many of my heroes stopped in to check out sales horses or just to bullshit. It was heady stuff for an 18-year-old with gigantic aspirations. *Is that so-and-so I've been idolizing via VHS memories of the '88 Olympics?* I was now riding more than grooming and no longer mucking stalls, making certain enemies of my envious roomies. I wasn't a full-fledged rider-trainer and I wasn't the barn help. I had no friends here. I belonged to my dreams and not much else.

To further earn their resentment, I eventually got access to the private lounge filled with trophies, photos, and other prized memorabilia. I spent my nights among the medals on display from the Olympics, Pan American Games, and World Cup victories. I watched endless tapes of heroic wins and sudden losses and studied every ride, pausing and rewinding over and over again, captivated and studious like I had never been before. If high school had been this exciting, I might have shown up for class between cocktails.

In mid-March, we filled a custom semi-tractor trailer with horses and headed to Arizona for the winter horse show circuit, our new home for the next two months. Grooming at a horse show is incredibly hard work. There is immense physical labor coupled with the need for attention to important details (each horse has its own show schedule, feed, medical, training program, and equipment requirements). Up at 5 am, getting horses ready and walking them between rings is a non-stop affair. My riding had been put on hold while I earned my way once again. I was cleaning stalls and feeding during breaks in the competition and too busy to catch a glimpse of the action in the show ring. At the end of the day we had dinner together and then it was back to the show stables for night check at 10 pm. Day to night and night to day was one interminable loop.

Once again, I eventually earned my way back on to the horses and got the opportunity to warm up some of my trainer's top mounts. My riding improved very quickly. This was a completely different level of excellence. I had gone from high school football to the NFL. The mindset and skillset at this level was truly Olympic.

The horse show itself was a different world entirely. We were stabled next to a private enterprise developed exclusively for two sisters, both under 11, and their nine show ponies. They flew home to attend school Monday through Wednesday and then flew back by private jet, with a nanny and tutor assigned to each of them, to ride at the show from Thursday through Sunday. This was 30 years before "remote learning." Their mom and dad had started a national pizza restaurant chain.

There were teens from South Korea who came to compete, sponsored by their family's international electronics conglomerate. One of the horses I groomed belonged to a Canadian who owned a number of television stations. I wasn't a professional groom or rider or owner. Once again, I found myself an alien in the ecosystem, with nowhere to plug in.

When you are immersed in this horse show world for long enough, your perception of money gets skewed. As I rode more and more and groomed less and less, I started to fit in. At least I thought I had. At one point, my boss got word about a show jumper for sale at a "great price." He encouraged me to try him out and I did. He was an incredible horse and I was jumping bigger jumps than I ever had, with ease! Pure endorphins.

That night, I couldn't wait to call back home. With my duties completed, I made the call to Mom and Dad from a payphone at the showgrounds. I told them all about this incredible horse and the rock bottom $120,000 price tag and begged them to buy him for me. *Surely they will get excited too and come up with the cash.* They sputtered. They mumbled. They stuttered. And then they burst out laughing. What was I thinking?! Surely I knew this wasn't even a possibility in any way. Had I gone crazy? *I'm not one of them and I do not belong here.* Reality set in once again in a complete adrenaline dump – if I was going to ride, it would continue to be on other people's horses.

The horse show experience ended with two life-changing events. The first was a failed drug test. Not mine, mind you. I was years away from my first dabble, and my drinking had been forced into submission because I had no cash and lived entirely on what I was fed. No, this was the failed drug test of a horse. I happened to walk up behind one of my heroes – an icon in the sport – as he was handing a big wad of cash to a horse show official, a drug testing official. I was heartbroken.

The second event took place days later when news broke about a criminal conspiracy to kill horses to collect large insurance payouts. There had been the intentional electrocution of horses using automatic water systems to make it look like an accident. There had been faked horse trailer accidents. I was devastated. This life I had longed for was not the pristine dreamland of horses and blue ribbons I had imagined.

I returned home from the apprenticeship and the bad news was quickly forgotten as I stepped into a busy assistant trainer position. I had left as an amateur and returned as a pro. Riding 12–14 horses a day, my job was to improve their performance for their owners. I was thrown on one, trained for 20–30 minutes, hopped off and handed the reins to a groom while I was thrown on the next one, almost in one motion. It was horse after horse after horse and then, in the afternoon, the junior riders would come after school for their lessons. Standing in the dirt in the sun, teaching young riders was rewarding but exhausting. And after hours of lessons with kids, the adults would show up for their lessons after work. At the end of the day, I could barely keep my eyes open on the drive home, my teeth covered in dust and my body completely spent. I loved every minute of it.

Until I didn't. The reality of a "lifelong love" becoming a "grueling job" was setting in. The horses were starting to irritate me and it was no longer fun. Instead of animals that brought me joy, they had become obstacles to overcome with various issues to fix. I had recently seen my heroes paying off drug testers and killing horses for money to make an impossible career possible. The dream was in doubt.

My best possible career scenario would be to find a benefactor to buy incredible horses so that I could live on the road competing at horse shows 300 days out of the year. And somehow, just as I was losing my love for the horse world, that exact opportunity presented itself in the form of a wonderful billionaire couple. They were caring and supportive and willing to help me reach my dreams. There was great potential there for a sponsorship of a lifetime.

But just as opportunity showed up, I began to see that the ending looked less like a dream and more like a disappointment. I briefly attempted to make a go of some investment horse scenarios and then fled the scene when things weren't working out. With my sudden selfish exit, I left a number of people worse off than when I found them. I didn't understand this until many years and many journal entries later. I had engaged in the same denial I had used to hide my sexual identity from myself. I had learned to keep in constant motion, never looking too closely at the wake of my decisions. I was OUT.

Where's the beef?

It's a funny thing when a dream come true turns into something you no longer want after all. It's probably sadder than dreams pursued and lost. The "what might have been" is perhaps a better tingle than that slow ache of a dream gone wrong. *What now? College? No. That would just be like more high school. I want to earn and find my place.* At the time, the best place to find a new dream was the classified ads. As I hunted, I came across an opportunity to apply for a management position with Arby's. After several interviews, I was given the assistant manager position at a store in central Denver. I was proud and excited about my new opportunity to find a place for my ambitions to call home.

I was immensely committed to success and read a new leadership book every week. I doubt there was another more committed assistant manager in the Arby's system. I had learned a strong work ethic and urge to compete during my time with the horses and this was relatively easy work in comparison. After all, my duties were inside, without sun or dust or 1,400-pound animals to negotiate with. This wasn't just an entry-level manager job to me. I saw this as a path to executive-level leadership in the larger corporation that owned this franchise. I saw wealth and power as my path to acceptance.

You could often find me in the store on my days off, cleaning up our parking lot, doing detailed cleanings of the trash cans, and clearing dirty syringes from the restrooms. *Oh, the disgusting junkies. Can't they find a better place to shoot up? Do they have no pride? Are they so lazy that they can't find a way out of their bad decisions? Pathetic.*

I was as zealous as an owner. This was my first crew. I relished leading the people, helping them grow and promoting them. Coaching and leadership came naturally to me (although I wouldn't have used these words to describe my role back then). Unfortunately, I did take my job just a tad too seriously. I was managing minimum-wage workers in a fast-food joint but acting like I was running IBM from the executive suite. As you can imagine, I was slightly irritating to my direct reports. The leadership lessons I was learning in books by authors such as Peter Drucker and Ken Blanchard were written for executives in large corporations, not a clueless first-time assistant manager in a fast-food restaurant.

There was a book I read once about a ruthless corporate takeover artist. He would fire 20% of the upper management team on his first day to establish his dominance and scare the rest of the executive suite into submission. This inspired me, and at the first challenge to my authority I gave one of my charges a serious written warning. It was clear insubordination. The guy had failed to clean the meat slicer properly and was refusing to go back and fix his error. Two days later, the same issue came up and, again, he refused to redo his work. I fired him on the spot in front of everyone. Kindness and empathy were nowhere to be found. It was a "get the hell out of my restaurant" kind of moment. I wasn't sad to see him go; I was excited. The power was a bit intoxicating. I had all the power, just like I did with the STP stickers and the vodka. I had what these people needed – employment. This was almost as good as belonging. At least I was in control. *They may not like me, but they better act like they do.*

Two days after his humiliating public termination, he appeared in the store to grab a Pepsi and say hi to his friends. I refused him service and asked him to leave immediately. He responded with a well-known finger gesture. I yelled at him from behind the counter to leave. Tempers flared. Name calling ensued. He jumped the counter in a rage, ready to kick my ass. Looking back, I think it would have been a well-deserved beating. Lucky for me, the fry guy intervened and held him off me. "Get out or I'll call the police." And so he left.

I didn't feel the power anymore. I felt the core of my gut telling me I had just behaved shamefully. My ex-employee was in the wrong in many ways, but I was the leader and I had failed to set an example. I had failed to display the character of a leader. I had failed to lead. Excellence must be pursued with vigor, but when our people fall short, they deserve honor, grace, and kindness. Lesson learned.

One day we ran out of roast beef. It was a far busier day than usual thanks to a nearby festival that attracted throngs of hungry visitors. The roast beef takes 5–6 hours to cook, so there was no quick fix even if I could get my hands on some. There were long lines of people waiting for us to serve what Arby's is known for: ROAST BEEF. We had none. I had underestimated the demand for the weekend and compounded the mistake with bad inventory management. It was a customer service nightmare and I was thoroughly humiliated in front of my crew. It was a LONG day. Leaders are measured against the tough stuff – when stuff goes wrong. The roast beef buck stops here. Lesson learned.

One day, while working the drive-thru as I did every Sunday, I met a guy. A dreamer always, I knew there was a bigger dream than being Arby's district manager. Any time someone drove through in a nice car, I made a habit of asking them what they did for a living. This guy was in a brand-new Acura and it shined. Sleek, fancy, expensive. "What do you do for work?" I asked. "Stockbroker," he said as he winked, grabbed his food, shouted, "Keep the change, kid," and sped off. I knew instantly that I was going to be a stockbroker. While my friends were suckered into getting college degrees, I'd be making my first million. I'd go to New York and make it big doing stock breaking things.

Stock breaking

Back to the classifieds, I saw the help wanted ad: *Stockbrokers. No experience necessary – will train. Career night.*

I went to career night and heard all about Ferraris, mansions, and helping people reach financial freedom while I reached mine. I interviewed with them the next week. They required a personality test, but they "accidentally" left a sample test with sample answers. I dutifully fell in line and scored with the ideal personality to be a stockbroker with this firm.

One important part of that ideal personality – being straight as hell. It was very clear that this job would require an impenetrable closet. Back I went.

In my eagerness to fit in, I didn't even pause to realize that I was cheating the personality test. It was my dream, really. I finally had the secret code for how to fit in! They agreed to sponsor me for the securities exam; all I had to do was study and pass. I quit Arby's and got a job close to the building where the classes were held. I would work at KFC during the day and walk right over to the classes at night.

This KFC had a salad bar and my job was to keep it stocked. I studied for the securities exam on all my breaks, lunches, and late into the night. If I didn't pass the test, fast food would be my future. I didn't have money for a second attempt.

I had spent my entire grocery budget for the exam prep classes, and KFC management didn't provide shift meals like they had at Arby's. I ate all I could while restocking from the walk-in refrigerator, secretly stealing potato salad, bacon bits, and chocolate pudding in hurried spoonfuls, right out of the oversized tubs.

Somehow I passed the exam on my first try and left KFC behind. I was going to be a rich stockbroker, significant at last. The world would have to let me in. If necessary, I would buy my way in.

After two weeks of training, I reported to my first day of work on the trading floor at 6 am. We had motivational meetings every morning, led by the sales manager. We were all expected to be on the floor before 6 am and, right on time, the door would SLAM open and Kent would explode through the row of desks, virtually floating to the front of the room. An ex-NFL pro, he was young and powerful and I was in awe of his custom suits and incredible energy. *How can anyone be this enthusiastic this early in the day?!*

Cocaine. Lots and lots of corner office cocaine. That's how.

I was too naive, inspired, enthusiastic to notice.

We were taught to cold call through the phone book, seeking investors from the right zip codes to "take a sizable position" in one of our firm's penny stock offerings. Airship Enterprises Ltd, founded by Lou Pearlman, was a featured stock in our trades. The stock traded as high as $6 and later to 3 cents before the company was shut down. Mr. Pearlman also founded the boy band NSYNC. Later, he was convicted of running a massive Ponzi scheme. Busy guy. He died in federal prison serving a 25-year sentence. These were the types of characters our firm raised capital for.

The company I worked for had been formed after Blinder, Robinson & Company was closed. The CEO, Meyer Blinder, had gone to prison for racketeering, securities fraud, and money laundering. Think *Wolf of Wall Street* and you get the idea. My bosses had slid out from under that particular rock and came together to create this new firm. I had no clue.

I fully bought the coked-up sales propaganda each morning and I burned through the phone book. I was here to please my leaders, earn big fat commission checks, and maybe even help a few investors along the way. The trouble was, it was tough to get someone on the phone and even tougher to get them to buy stock. We were taught every cold-calling, hard-selling phone manipulation trick imaginable.

"You need more energy, Muller. Get on your fucking desk and let me see you jumping up and down." And so I did. Standing on my desk, my head through a hole where the drop ceiling used to be, I was yelling, "Who wears the pants in your family?!" The poor guy on the sucker end of the phone had suggested he wanted to talk to his wife before going ahead with a stock purchase. Needless to say, he bought the stock. Needless to say, he canceled the purchase the next day. Smart guy.

This was supposed to be the American dream. I truly believed I was selling financial freedom. I wanted to deliver on those dreams for my customers (I think I managed to get two customers) and for myself, too. I wanted to upgrade my RTD bus pass and thrift store suit to a Mercedes and Armani. I wanted to look the part, feel the part, and *be a part of something.*

After about 12 weeks, I was starting to get the drift. There were only three or four (out of 50 or so) stockbrokers making any money. And they were the ones who made me want to bathe in bleach any time they came within ten feet of me. I started spending more time in the bathroom with the *Wall Street Journal*, hiding from the phone. I started wondering why we never had happy clients showing up to the offices.

The place was more like a locker room – sexist, homophobic, racist, vile. I did my best straight guy impression and hoped beyond hope that I wouldn't get found out. I would be booted immediately. *Goddamnit, I'm so ashamed. Please don't figure out who I really am.*

One night, while they were airing the last episode of *Cheers* and the entire nation was watching TV, we were all on the phones cold calling, undeterred by what was practically a national holiday. We were selling a new issue stock that the firm had underwritten. Boy, were people unhappy to get that call! "But sir, I wouldn't have called you now, of all times, unless this was a truly life-changing stock." I believed every word. Some of us were successful selling this .07-cent stock. After a few days of hard selling, with all the bosses screaming from the corner office, the stock rose dramatically to almost a dollar. This was a life-changing profit for our customers – all within a few days.

But when it came time to sell the stock in order for our customers to capture the profit, no one on the trading floor could get a trade through. All busy signals. By the time we could, the stock was closer to 2 cents, never to rise again. This, I would later learn, was a classic "pump and dump" scheme. The firm owned a HUGE amount of the stock. They didn't execute trades as instructed by clients but let the buy orders accumulate instead (this is a big no-no). Then they executed the buy orders in rapid succession. With few total shares on the market (a small float), the stock rose dramatically. "Small float, gonna POP!" Then the company sold their huge position at a massive profit, driving the stock back to below where it was. The company won big time, and the customers were left holding the worthless bag. Once I saw this play out, it was the last straw. I was willing to cold call and denigrate myself to make it big, and I was all about the most selfish way to get there, but I wasn't willing to cross this fraudulent line.

I loved the unlimited upside of this job. I was all in for the fast money. But I had no money and I didn't want to be a criminal. It was clear I didn't belong.

At 21, I was a stock trading burnout. It was the end of the line for my big money, big status dreams.

CHAPTER 4.
CULTURES AND VULTURES

It broke my heart to leave another dream behind and take a job at Charles Schwab. They offered a salary and benefits and much less upside than the penny stock scam, but I had to eat and I didn't want to be a criminal. I felt like a sell-out – a multimillionaire in the making turned order-taker, consigned to a sea of cubicles.

It was like abandoning the strip club for the symphony. No more elbows and assholes on the trading floor. This was Fortune 500 polish with rules and standards and an actual HR department. I didn't miss the fear-driven commission frenzy, but I mourned the adrenaline rush. My new broker class spent the first three months in rigorous training that was a college-level crash course in the financial markets. It turns out I knew nothing but how to cold call in a frenzy while the bosses manipulated the markets.

We were tethered to security badges now, and locker room banter was replaced by a gentler corporate etiquette. The toxic bro was still here, he was just screening the room more carefully before launching into offensives. My high school diploma was surrounded by college degrees and MBAs. Having just turned 22, I was younger than the rest – I was not like the others. As always.

Every two weeks, I got a direct deposit. The checks were never late and they never bounced. The leaders didn't scream or jump up and down. And if there was cocaine and prostitutes, it wasn't happening out in the open or in the corner office.

My class of broker recruits was hired to field incoming calls from Schwab customers that were trading their own accounts. Online trading hadn't quite arrived, so we were the computers, accepting buy and sell orders for stocks, mutual funds, and options. We were the machines in a huge call center during a massive bull market, part of an epic hiring spree to keep up with unrelenting demand.

But in April 1994, just as our class was released from training and turned over for trading, the market took a dip and pause. The phones stopped ringing. The gigantic trading operation spanning several entire floors went quiet. A gentle hum of disappointment whispered to me as I took my seat with my new team of 23 other stockbrokers. The Nerf footballs, once used to calm the nerves of overworked brokers, were now being tossed back and forth from team to team in the dead sea. There were jokes, less inappropriate but still sexist, racist, and homophobic enough to alert me to the ever-present dangers. I was welcome. In the closet.

My class had been integrated into existing teams and I was the only newbie "Schwabbie" in my group. I was young enough that questions about my marital status, kids, etc., were easily bounced back with careful banter aimed at practiced misdirection. It was clear – I wasn't like them. I knew I couldn't easily join in their games of Nerf football catch. The only thing I could catch was a cold. Any time the footballs flew in my direction, I ducked out of habit, just like I had on the baseball field. *Isn't that the sane thing to do when something is heading right at you?!* As the reality set in that this was going to be a slow period that might last more than a couple of days, the footballs seemed to sail with more force. They drilled in tight spirals that I couldn't catch and I certainly couldn't recreate. The only spiral I could perform was on ice skates.

Playing defense, I sat in my cube, head down and out of sight, and I read. I studied our trading manuals, I devoured the content, I memorized the stock symbols and formulas, and I learned as much as I could. I kept my head down and I answered my colleague's unspoken questions for them: *Something's different about this guy. What is it? Oh, he's a nerd. He's a workaholic. He's a brown-noser. But he's safe. No threat to me or my tenuous masculinity.*

I was desperately ambitious and quickly singled out as a serious employee on the fast track. Using work to hide who I was helped me leapfrog my football classmates. I accepted a lateral transfer to a swing shift team, working 3 pm to midnight in return for a 10% pay differential. I knew this shift was smaller and I could swim more successfully toward a bigger-fish-smaller-pond strategy.

The market began to rebound, the call volume followed, and I served up high customer service survey scores and accurate trades – the two most important measures in this job. In the transactional phone calls aimed at building or reducing stock positions in portfolios, I found humanity wherever I could. Clients would call and ask us to read news on companies (truly the olden days), get stock quotes, and then discuss strategy. We were impartial and weren't allowed to give advice, but the conversations were always compelling.

I made it a game to find out something interesting about every person that called. It made the work more fun, and it created much higher customer satisfaction scores. My scores reflected the connection established on the call. The human connection. I could flub the news story, stumbling over my words. I could repeat the trade back incorrectly only to be corrected. If we connected as people, from their home to my cube and back again, then my scores soared.

In the cracks between the trades and the moments between quotes, there was human life. I loved connecting with those faceless voices, jumping from one call to the next, mood to mood, fear to greed and back again, around the bend to a sense of humor or perhaps a sense of superiority. Sometimes the calls for quotes and news were really calls for companionship, a cry to end the lonely night.

I was grateful for those calls because I was lonely, too. I couldn't seem to make any friends at work. It was just like that playground from my childhood. This time the guys were talking about game stats and hitting averages, but I was still a foreigner in this land. I had outgrown my accent, but not my differences.

Charles Schwab himself had a dearly beloved gay assistant who died in the '80s at the start of the AIDS epidemic. Schwab was supportive of the gay community in many ways, financial and otherwise, and I learned that the San Francisco headquarters was teeming with "family." I had pushed myself back into the closet when I hit the hostile scene at the penny stock firm, but Schwab was starting to feel like a safer place. And then, on the swing shift, I quickly learned I was still living in the land of heteronormative rule and it would be best if I didn't bring *all of me* to work.

Our team manager was a die-hard "Schwabbie," and he was enthusiastic about sharing his knowledge. He was patient and supportive. He loved the company, loved the work, and loved his team. But he also loved the "homo" jokes, often laughing about so-and-so who seemed "a little light in the loafers." It was a common late-night refrain as the calls sometimes slowed and the team reverted to banter. *If you are going to get promoted to the next level, this guy is your ticket. He holds the power. Follow the clues. Fall in line. Fit in.* And so I did. I played the bachelor role even though I was six years into a fully committed relationship. Surely it can't be healthy to spend your life pretending to be someone you're not?

I didn't have much time to think through the trauma I was creating by living in shame and denial. We were barely able to keep up with the call volume. Much of our work in those days was providing stock quotes for investors curious about their stock positions. Quoting prices was considered busy work by management. The calls didn't require market knowledge or experience, so they were a waste of our securities licenses. We simply entered a stock symbol into the machine and it would spit out a quote. Management quickly devised a plan to hire 100 temps to provide stock quotes. My manager asked if I would like to train and supervise the temps, and suddenly I had 100 people reporting to me at Charles Schwab. My homophobic manager had recognized my ambitions, my hard work, and my diligent studying. Lesson learned. Be who they want you to be and you will rise.

The employment agency sent us 100 temps and, by the first break, I had cut about 30% of them for showing up late, goofing off, etc. By lunch, we would cut another 20% for not learning quickly enough. It took a few weeks of binge hiring and training until we finally had about 100 temps, on the phones, providing stock quotes. I was thrilled with training and supervising them. This temporary quoter position was an opportunity for the temps to eventually come on full time at the firm. This was a big opportunity, especially for someone working a minimum wage temporary position. It was fun to pick out the temps that should go on for further training to customer service rep positions. It was meaningful and rewarding to find the motivated, the earnest, the winners and offer them recognition and opportunity.

The supervisory experience with the temps served up the next opportunity for me, too, and close to my one-year anniversary at Schwab, I applied for a team manager position and was selected. At 23, I was running a team of 24 stockbrokers, all of them better educated than me. I experienced a serious case of impostor syndrome in management training, trying to figure out why I had any business managing these people who, until very recently, had been my more experienced peers. I arrived at work two hours early every day. I remained long after my last team member had punched the clock. I turned my 8-hour shift into a 12- to 13-hour shift. Every day. I spent my day off studying team building and leadership books. I cured my impostor syndrome with new expertise. My drive to go hard was my friend. I hated school but I loved learning so I created my own college in real time.

It paid off. Our team hit such high service and productivity numbers that Chuck Schwab himself sat with us during a visit to

Denver. He was there to figure out what the heck we were doing to hit these numbers. Many of my brokers were promoted out of that team and I got my first taste of what it means to succeed "through others."

I was bringing my love for the consumer, developed from countless hours on the phone with clients, to my team. Service delivery creates loyalty and builds the brand. Even at a massive company, this happens one conversation at a time. Trading stock over the phone requires precision and careful attention to detail. That technical groundwork must be covered first. But once the proficiency sets those smooth transactions in motion, the gold at the end of the business rainbow is in the client touchpoints.

Charles Schwab understood this service ethic and taught it to me. The customer service surveys drove our individual and team bonuses and it showed. We had a culture that cared for the clients beyond their investment portfolios. I became fanatical about finding new ways to get those calls to create the best possible client experience. I listened to hundreds of hours of recorded conversations. As a team, we fine-tuned our approaches, gathering tips culled from careful study of those calls. We built a tight culture of excellence and obsession with service on our team. Somehow we ended up with our own language and shorthand and inside jokes. We were a tight unit and we cared about each other.

Champagne dreams

A year into that position, I was given my next promotion to a senior manager role. I had developed a relationship during several months of morning smoke breaks with an executive that ran Schwab One, the banking side of the business. They offered checking and debit cards tied to brokerage accounts. Recently transferred from the San Francisco HQ, Leslie was incredibly smart and cool and a LONG time Schwabbie. Somehow she just knew I was gay and it wasn't a thing. I could be myself with her and that was exhilarating. Plus, she knew so much. I learned and learned during our casual smoky conversations and, when she posted a job for the senior manager role, I jumped at the chance to work with her.

I got the job. I was the first one to apply. I was probably the only one to apply.

At the time, Schwab One was in the midst of some growing pains and there was a lot of work to be done. I relished the challenge. This wasn't just the deep end of the pool for me; I had jumped into a lake and it was on fire. I was 24, with four managers reporting to me, each of them running a team of customer service and operations reps. I reported directly to Leslie and she took me to business school over the next few years. She was a once-in-a-lifetime mentor to me and we quickly became friends.

We spent long hours after work nursing vodka tonics and discussing business and life at the nearby Irish pub happy hour. Our conversations ranged from Schwab corporate politics to life goals and everything in between. I made it very clear that I wanted to be a VP and a millionaire by 30. She asked me why, gently suggesting that a goal unconnected to a greater purpose might not be fulfilling. There was a lesson there that I wasn't ready to learn.

The goal for Leslie and me was clear – Leslie gets promoted to VP and then I get promoted to director. Leslie came close and then, instead of promoting her, they assigned a VP from HQ that she would report to. This VP managed to kill almost all the love in that department. We were required to submit insanely detailed daily state-of-the-business reports to him. It took four or five hours every day for me and my managers to compile and balance the numbers. It made no sense. We were so busy with the state-of-the-business reports that we couldn't *run* the business. Everything and everyone suffered.

We protested but it was useless. Service to consumers didn't matter to HQ now, only numbers did. Leslie and I knew we just had to outlast this clown. Eventually we did. Again, Leslie was up for a promotion. Again, she was passed over, and this time a local VP was hired from the outside to preside over the department.

She was the worst type of corporate shark and was clearly there to push Leslie out, and Leslie was smart enough to see around the corner at the oncoming collision and resigned.

It was clear I was left exposed politically with Leslie gone and a new VP that wanted to shake things up to solidify her power base (just as I had done at Arby's). She was smoother and smarter than I had been but just as brutal. I had been in the senior manager job for two years, but experience didn't matter like it once had. Schwab had doubled in size during my tenure. Corporate politics was snuffing out the meritocracy. My work ethic and dedication didn't hold much weight either. It didn't make up for my lack of a college degree. In my four years at Schwab, we had transitioned from a culture of customer focus to a culture of metrics focus. People were routinely sacrificed to the altar of operational efficiency.

I got tired of slamming my head against the proverbial writing on the wall. The message was clear – there was no place for me in the new Schwab. I felt trapped. Where could I possibly replace my very comfortable salary as a 26-year-old college drop out? I was stuck, and so I found every miserable way to undermine the new boss of Schwab One. It was a passive-aggressive campaign that so many unhappy corporate disappointments wage quietly against their captors. It's probably the cause of many trillions in lost profits. But I was powerless and hopeless.

And then the internet came calling.

PART TWO: DYING OF ACHIEVEMENT

CHAPTER 5.
BOOM!

I had just about given up all hope of a director-level job (the step between senior manager and VP by the age of 30) after the sad exit of my last boss and the disruptive entrance of my current one. She brought her own people with her and it was suffocating. For the first time since I had been at Schwab, resourcefulness, ingenuity, and work ethic didn't seem to matter. It was all about where you got your degree (or, in my case, where you didn't get a degree). Clearly, I no longer fitted in.

Then the headhunter called.

"I'm running a search for a venture capital-backed Silicon Valley software startup. We need to fill a director of client services position for their internet division in Denver. Are you interested in learning more?"

"Absolutely not," I retorted, insulted that anyone would dare imply I lacked complete and total loyalty to my current road to executive stardom.

But by the next day something had shifted, and suddenly I had even less patience for my new boss. Just knowing there was a different possibility changed the way I looked at everything. Choices have that effect. I called the recruiter back and immediately secured an interview spot with the CEO of the software company. He was in town from San Francisco, hiring for key director positions for the division.

We met in a hotel lobby. I was dressed in my best suit and tie and he was in jeans and a t-shirt. This was long before the cliché tech CEO uniform became a cliché. I was shocked and, for a minute, I worried that he wasn't for real. The guy that interviewed me at Arby's was dressed better.

But as soon as he opened his mouth I knew that he was the right guy and I was in the right place at the right time. He had assembled some of the best and brightest tech minds and tech money and his software solved a big problem – how to manage the learning infrastructure for big enterprises. He had hired people from Oracle and Microsoft and raised many millions through Sequoia Capital, the same private-equity firm that funded Yahoo and Google. The Denver internet services division would take the software solution and apply it to the burgeoning online marketplaces.

It was an easy interview, really a non-interview. I spoke about my experience running a 50-person service and operations department and his response was simply, "Well, I know Charles Schwab only hires the brightest." That was it. I was told to expect an offer letter the next day and, sure enough, it arrived as promised.

I almost lost my lunch when I opened the letter, and that's not a figure of speech. I jumped so hard when I saw the numbers that my footlong sandwich almost fell from my lap. The salary was about 45% of what I was currently earning at Schwab. I had no interest in going backward like that.

But 16,000 shares. They were offering stock options that would give me the opportunity to buy 16,000 shares of stock at *17 cents per share*. The stock options were worthless at the time, of course, because the company hadn't even filed to go public. But the chance to leapfrog professionally and financially, while running from the dark blonde cloud that had descended over my life at Schwab, was just too enticing to pass up. This might be my big break. And these guys didn't care that I had dropped out of college; they wanted me for ME. My ambitious entrepreneurial streak would be welcomed, even rewarded, again. *I will fit in there.*

I took the job but I couldn't find the office building for my first day. The directions led me to an apartment building. *This can't be right.* After circling a few more times, I knocked on the door and my new colleague answered the door to her apartment, our "Denver HQ." We didn't even have office space yet.

There were a few people sitting around staring at laptop screens and a couple meeting around a whiteboard on an easel. I confidently announced myself from the front door, "I'm Grant, head of client services."

My new boss laughed, "Well, we don't have any clients yet, so you're also head of sales."

"Great. What are we selling?"

"Dunno. Our software is built to manage the learning and education departments for massive organizations. We need to figure out what we can offer online to smaller companies, using that platform. You need to recruit our first 50 beta customers and we'll build whatever they need."

My first day was spent cold calling training companies out of the phone book, trying to get someone to take a meeting with me. This was not the high-tech venture capital-backed glamour I had signed up for. I had expected a big private office enclosed in glass and somewhere chic. This was more like donuts for lunch and working through dinner.

I was not happy about cold calling again, but over the next several months I successfully brought in some beta clients that helped us define what the market needed. Ultimately, we were building e-commerce stores for small training companies. I built a core team of talented telesales reps and, by the end of the year, we were beginning to roll out our offering.

At the same time, the company was building momentum toward an IPO (initial public offering). A buzz started to build in the office (we had finally moved into a little office suite in an actual office building). My calculator was busy multiplying 16,000 shares by some optimistic stock prices. I was shopping for Ferraris on the internet.

Things were looking up, with one exception: I *hated* every single minute of the work. The sales were business-to-business sales and essentially we were selling a commodity. It was more like selling tech support than an actual service. I was miserable. I missed the consumer. I missed the true human connections. There was no relationship, just bits and bytes exchanged for money.

The tech went straight over my head. For the first time in my life, I doubted my intelligence, but I was too insecure to simply say, "I don't get it, teach me." I figured that my inability to read Java like the rest of the guys was a lack of intelligence rather than a lack of skill. Looking back, I realize I was out of my element, but if I had approached the problem from a skillset perspective I could have figured it out. Instead, I took it as a familiar sign that I didn't belong. I had no business being there at all.

Then we went public.

My thousands of shares at 17 cents each were now worth $60 a piece. There was a jubilant frenetic energy in the office. We had young internet developers working around the clock to meet impossible targets, and we were all stacking some serious paper profits in the stock market. We moved into a new gargantuan office suite in a better building. The design was tech-forward stunning. When you stepped off the elevator, it was as if you were walking right into our website – same colors and shapes. Our kitchen was fully stocked and breakfast/lunch/dinner was catered. Car detailers came to shine all the new sports cars in the lot. A barber visited to cut what was left of my hair. I had a foosball table right outside my office. It was all set up so that we never wanted to leave, working longer and longer hours. Why leave, after all, if everything you need is right there?

This was long before Google popularized this campus work environment. We were showing up to work in jeans and t-shirts. I remember the way that the other tenants in the building would look down their noses at us when we stepped onto the elevator – that is, until the elevator doors opened, revealing our suite.

That's right, you middle-aged suburbanites drowning in mediocrity. Stop judging my jeans and t-shirt. I just made more on our IPO than you will make in the next ten years!

Play time

As hard as we worked, we played pretty damn hard too. I had spent my life drinking enthusiastically, routinely getting blind drunk as a high school kid. At Schwab, that old habit reared its ugly head – and in high gear. I drove home many nights blind drunk. The type of drunk where you have to close one eye to find the center line. I had quietly started to drink again. My partner and I had agreed to drink socially. I took massive bucketful gulps of booze when he wasn't looking. And I drank any time I could at business and social gatherings. I was still a drunk; there was no question. But under the controlling watch of my partner, I managed to manage the unmanageable. Achievement and success and money and the obsession with metrics that Schwab shoved down my throat had filled the liquor niche until then, but drinking was back in the house and had kicked out the guests.

Until then, I had always steered clear of drugs. I didn't even touch marijuana. But now, working in high tech – and for some reason I don't remember – I made an exception one night. I took an ecstasy pill at the club (who doesn't want ECSTASY?!).

It was everything "getting high" should feel like. It was a warm glow of love and sex and joy and ultimate acceptance in pill form. It was that feeling you get when you yawn as the sun hits your face. It was a long slow orgasm while you're drinking a chocolate shake and I wanted more.

I fell into my own personal club circuit routine – hit the gay club around 10 pm, drink up, then drive drunk to the after-hours club at 1 am or so, take a pill, and dance until 5 am. When

I wasn't dancing, I would sit on the booming floor speakers enveloped by bass.

Ecstasy was the perfect drug for me; it almost always provided a truly euphoric high with no side effects. This isn't the case for everyone. Some people go into a depression when they come down from ecstasy. I didn't. As my pill wore off, I was released into the gentle early afternoon, refreshed and renewed as if I had just left a spa day.

I tried two pills. I tried twice a week. I tried back-to-back nights. I tried one while I was coming down off another. But no matter how much I took or how often, one pill, once a week, for one high (varying in intensity based on my own chemistry and the pill's exact contents) was all that worked.

One night, my friends and I took separate cars from the gay club to the after-hours club. I took my pill on the way and, by the time I pulled up, I was so high that I didn't leave the car, or move the car, until the sun came up. I just sat there in pure thrilling bliss for several hours. "High" is named after moments like this. It was the most amazing feeling I have ever had. I was high in the heavens. From that moment on, I was on the chase. *I MUST HAVE MORE.*

Because I only used the drug once a week, there were no immediately noticeable negative consequences. As I started to immerse myself in the ecstasy drug culture, I recognized a fellow hobbyist in one of my coworkers. He was going to similar clubs, listening to similar music, and came to work dressed for the club. After dancing around the topic for a bit, it became clear that he was not just a hobbyist but a serious practitioner with some important connections. Pills were in high demand at the club, and sometimes they were impossible to find. My friend at work solved this problem. Now, I could order more pills from him and plan ahead. Much more civilized than hunting and pecking at the club at 2 am.

Miserable all week at work, I started taking weekend trips to check out the club scene in different cities (New York, Los

Angeles, San Francisco). It was a fun change of scenery. And I didn't have to worry about finding pills, thanks to my new supply.

As the year 2000 fast approached, I planned a trip to a huge party in San Francisco with a friend. We stayed in an imaginative boutique hotel to ring in the new year in style. Each suite had been decorated by a different celebrity. We chose a corner suite designed by a horror movie maker.

Twenty-three years later, the irony finally becomes clear.

At some point late into the first night, cocaine came out of my buddy's pocket. He laid out a couple of cute, innocent white lines on the dresser. As if it was the most natural thing in the world, he breathed in the first line. *Voilà.* Soupy drunk and invincible, I dutifully vacuumed up the second one, which clearly had my name on it.

That was the beginning and the end of me. In that moment, my entire life switched from *before* to *after.* All was well. I was full and complete. I needed no one. I needed nothing. For the first time ever, I was content and at peace. And for the first time ever, I belonged just as I am.

I was no longer drunk. I wanted to run, climb, and dance. *Oh, holy fuck, I must DANCE!* "Let's go back to the club. They're still open for another hour." No response. I looked over at my friend. He had laid out a couple more lines and promptly passed out. He wasn't used to drinking like I did and he had kept up with me all night like a champ. Apparently, even the coke couldn't refresh him. There and then, I initiated a long-standing tradition of ignoring the pain of others in pursuit of my own pleasure. I did the two lines, rushed out of the room, and hailed a cab before the bellman could.

I was off in a taxi on the way back to the club to squeeze as much as I could out of the last hour of the night. "Faster, faster, faster," I was yelling at the cabbie as he launched from one steep San Francisco street to the next. "GODDAMNIT. GO, MOTHERFUCKER!" It was maddening that the car wouldn't lift off the streets like I expected it to.

In spite of the cab not transforming into a helicopter, I made it back to the club and, just as I hit the dance floor, I learned an important lesson about coke: You will always need more. Soon. I was starting to come down. This was not the all-night party I was accustomed to with ecstasy.

The coke high requires a regular, careful feeding. In coke land, you are always arriving at the party just in time to leave to do more. You are always making the grand entrance (in your mind) only to sneak off to the bathroom every few minutes. And when I started to come down, I started to feel sketchy. Self-conscious. Dirty. I slithered back to the hotel room and did what was left of my friend's stash. The sun was rising on January 1, 2000.

In one night's moment, I was consumed. I was owned and I knew it. I was monosyllabic. M.O.R.E.

Back to work a day later than promised, it seemed as if I wasn't missed. It was the first week of a new century and, after a few days of pretend work (pushing emails around and taking too many smoke breaks), the weekend finally arrived.

We hit the Saturday night gay club, the after-hours club until 5 am, and then (without rest or sleep) the Sunday "tea dance," a gay daytime dance party. The ecstasy was losing its shine as the afternoon wore on, and we stopped at my condo for booze to compensate.

Thoroughly liquored and with no food in sight, we headed out for a 5 pm "brunch" at a local hotspot where we were regulars. I was daydreaming about my cocaine adventure from the prior weekend. When our favorite server asked me, "Will there be anything else?" I quipped, "Yes, please. I would like some cocaine."

She returned within five minutes and dropped an almost empty box of Marlboro Lights next to my plate.

"Leave $40 more for the tip," she said nonchalantly and walked away.

I was in shock. This wasn't an '80s movie, but somehow, at brunch, I had scored my own coke as if it were a doggy bag of leftovers. More importantly, I had scored my very first coke dealer.

CHAPTER 6.
BUST

I had a direct line to cocaine now, a hotline of sorts: 1-800-get-coke. My server-turned-dealer was happy to sell me $50 bags here and there. Within a few weeks, though, here and there turned to always and everywhere. At first it was a gentle nudge in the back of my mind – *I bet this party would be a little more fun with a bump of coke* or *Blasting the music while I'm cleaning is good, but I bet a bump of coke would make cleaning a whole lot more entertaining.* Coke made me brave and confident and sure socially.

I began to suspect that my new dealer was avoiding my calls; her service levels couldn't meet my new demands. I became concerned that she seemed to take her restaurant job too seriously, and this limited her availability to me. At the outset, I was meeting up with her on a Friday night for a $50 bag, but recently I had been calling her during the week as well. When my calls became too frequent, she resigned from her position as my inaugural cocaine attendant, and I was left with a blossoming habit and no supply.

At work the next week, I casually mentioned to my ecstasy pill colleague that my tastes were expanding, and he introduced me to Alberto, my first true coke "connection." Dealers (think wholesale) that carry serious weight – kilos/pounds – are heavily armed, violent, and paranoid, and they will stick out like a sore thumb in your favorite high-end sushi restaurant. A connection (think retailer) buys directly from those scary characters and tends to deal in ounces. They package those ounces into smaller retail quantities and earn the markup, just like any other retailer. That way, hobby users, as I was, can maintain access to the drug without leaving their safe neighborhoods and without the need to interact with unsavory and unsafe characters.

Alberto was the perfect retail connection. He sold to suburbanites and professors, attorneys and doctors. He sold to those of us who consumed politely – your upper-middle-class-gentlemen cocaine users.

He drove a stylish BMW, lived in a nice neighborhood, and frequented the best restaurants. It was easy to pull up car to car in a parking lot to make a quick exchange. Two gentlemen in an upscale part of town – must be a couple of friends catching up or exchanging opera tickets or something. In fact, "ticket" was the code. "Hey, Alberto. I need a ticket to the show. Where will you be tonight around 7?" If he was out to dinner when I called, it was simple to stroll in to see him at a nice restaurant, two friends bumping into each other accidentally. He'd slip a packet of coke into my blazer side pocket and the quick handshake took care of the cash payment. It was that easy, and easy access makes for easy habits.

I was only partying on the weekends at this point. I would pick up on Friday after work, party through Sunday night, then get up on Monday to get the work week going. Everything was well in hand. My responsibilities were nicely managed on the weekdays. Except Monday. Calling in sick on Monday became a bit of an issue.

In an attempt to rectify this minor scheduling snafu, I tried starting my weekends earlier – on Thursday night. I would take Friday off to get a start on the three-day weekend. But that turned into a four-day weekend pretty quickly. My weekends were now Thursday night through Monday night. That worked better.

When Tuesday came around, I knew I needed to show my face at work after four days. By 10 am, I would be running to my car for a quick bump. Just to pick me up a bit. I was out again by 11 for an early lunch, spent in a nearby parking garage with my head in my lap vacuuming lines until I couldn't see straight. I would get so jacked up at lunch that I had to spend two hours coming back to Earth (I later learned that a couple shots of vodka would do the trick more efficiently). I would get back to work by 2 or so until 3, when I needed another "cigarette break."

One Friday, I met Alberto at his house. I bought an 8-ball of coke. An 8-ball is three and a half grams, which is an eighth of an ounce, hence the name. As per usual, I set up a few lines on a CD case as soon as I got in the car and snorted them in Friday traffic on the way home. *Don't mind me, Denver traffic. Just looking for something in my lap.*

But this time I didn't make it home; I didn't have the patience to wait. Frustrated with the little bits I could do while driving, I found a grocery store parking lot and finished the rest. I want MORE NOW. ALL OF IT.

I called Alberto. "Hey, I'm out of candy and on my way back." When I got to his place, he was super pissed, thinking I was selling the stuff without his okay. He couldn't fathom I had done that much that fast.

But then he took one look at me and knew I really *had* done that much on the way home. I was on a trajectory only he could see at that point. This was not a casual cocaine relationship anymore. I was clearly head over heels.

Suddenly, my dedicated drug dealer found a conscience and refused to sell me any more that night. He was convinced I was going to kill myself, either via an overdose or a car crash. I wasn't playing by the unwritten rules. I was a liability for him.

I left. Livid. Thirty minutes later, I was back and banging on his door. No call. No pleasantries. Irate. "Sell me more fucking coke now. Do your fucking job." He relented, with a promise from me that I'd wait to do more until I got home. I did so much when

I got home that I passed out with my ass in the air and my face on the coffee table. This is commonly called being "over-amped." My body was betraying me, shutting down to save me from death.

When I came to, I realized it was time I got honest with myself. This was not okay. This was no way to live. I simply couldn't go on like this, with a dealer that didn't have the dedication I needed to keep the coke flowing at a reasonable pace. It was time to find a better source.

By this time, I had dozens of new friends. I was very popular. I lived a block from a nightclub and, at closing time, I had taken to inviting people to my place for an "after party." Go-go dancers, drag queens, DJs, bartenders, all were welcome. At first, the parties were just about keeping the alcohol flowing, which I was happy to oblige, while I secretly did coke in my bedroom.

As I got to know some people better, we started having after-after parties. The general crowd would leave and I'd be left with my VIP crowd, huddled in a living room with velvet curtains pulled to block out the sun and house music blaring to block out the annoying chirping of the birds. We would snort the day away and, pretty soon, I realized that some of them were willing to keep the supply flowing if I could keep the cash flowing. I obliged.

I remember ripping a full-length mirror from the back of my guest bathroom door one morning, throwing it on the kitchen counter, and making lines that ran its length. *I wonder if this one will finally fucking kill me.* I think it nearly did. I must not have been out that long because, when I got pulled back to my feet, the other line was still there, untouched. I made light of the episode, chopped the line into smaller pieces for everyone else, then did more than my fair share of the smaller lines, pretending I didn't notice.

Party fouls like this were quickly forgiven when I had large quantities of cocaine for people to feed on. Not only did I fit in, but people had to fit in with ME. It was the STP stickers all over again. As long as I held the bag, I made the rules and I ran the show. If I put out a line for you as a guest in my house, you finished the line or you didn't get any more. I meant it, too. It was a desperate attempt to bring those around me down to my level of depravity. I needed people to use at my level to normalize my behavior.

But these club friends weren't willing to keep it up for long. When they all returned to their families and jobs at 6 am one Monday morning, I realized I would need to find new friends. *What is wrong with them, walking away from free drugs?!* I wanted the wretched and the fucked up around me. I needed to relate. Something darker had found its way in.

(Not) employee of the year

Meanwhile, back at the office, I dutifully showed up for the "work week" on Tuesday after another bout with "a nasty 24-hour stomach bug" on Monday. My lack of focus, interest, and presence was raising eyebrows. Our senior vice president flew in from Silicon Valley for a little chat. While in town, he suggested we go to dinner and I was quite convinced I was getting a nice raise.

Before we had ordered our dinner, my boss jumped right in. "Grant, what the hell is happening with you? I'm getting calls and emails about you. Half the time you're missing from action and the other half you're erratic. Your team is reporting disturbing behavior and your colleagues have given up trying to collaborate with you."

We had just successfully launched a massive new website. I had stayed up all night with the developers, the quality assurance folks, and my client support team to ensure that everything went off flawlessly. And it did. Yes, I had discreetly ventured to the restroom a little more than normal for some quick bumps to keep on my toes, but nothing noticeable. My boss had received a different report: "Grant spent half the night in the bathroom. Each time he reappeared, he was more erratic and bizarre. By the time we were launching the site, he had isolated himself in his office, where he was babbling to himself incoherently."

My colleagues, who had become friends, were worried about me. They wanted me to pull my own weight. Fuck them. Traitors.

I told my boss what he wanted to hear and he flew back to San Francisco, problem solved. I laid low for a bit. Well, until the weekend. I had a trip planned to a party in Los Angeles.

I was due back in the office on Monday morning, but it was Monday at 10 am and I was still in California, in a limo with two very unsavory characters I had just spent a sleepless weekend with. *THIS IS NOT GOOD.* I hit the coke for inspiration and quickly developed a plan – call in a bomb threat to the airline. This would explain why I had missed my flight the night before. "Get me to a pay phone NOW," I screamed to the driver. The limo slammed its screaming brakes and I hopped out to make the bomb threat call to the airline. As I tumbled (literally) out of the limo and stumbled to the pay phone, reality hit. Calling in a bomb threat was not a good idea. A bomb threat today wouldn't explain my missed flight from yesterday. What was I thinking?!

Back at work on Wednesday, I got a call from the senior VP. I had decided that the best way to explain my absence on Monday and extend the party another day was to fake a bad illness. This time, I selected bronchitis.

"Grant, it's time for you to pack up. I need you out of the office in an hour. Please don't make me fly back to Denver to do this." I was being terminated. I could keep my vested stock options, but I was done. "You think you're firing me? You can't fire me. I'm a fucking millionaire and I'm fucking retiring. I'm 28, you stupid fucker. I'm half your old-ass age."

And that's how I became a millionaire and retired at 28. That was the story I told myself and anyone else that would listen. And I did have my 16,000 shares of stock, worth enough money to cover the rest of my life if invested wisely.

Spoiler – I didn't invest wisely. I called every month or so to exercise more shares to cover my excessive party expenses. My habit was requiring a very regular feeding and my lifestyle was costing $20–30k a month, depending on travel and which "friends" were along for the ride.

Every few weeks a check would bounce, and that meant calling to exercise shares to replenish the account.

It wasn't just my spending that was oversized. I kept a serving plate with a big mound of cocaine in my kitchen cabinet. And the vodka was oversized. One positive side effect of coke is a superpower ability to consume alcohol. My lifetime love of liquor was well nurtured during these cocaine times. I could drink and drink and drink without passing out, and I did so 24 hours a day. It was not unusual for me to go through a "family-size" bottle of vodka in 24 hours. "Ice is your best mixer" – my vodka tonics were replaced by vodka on ice.

I had filled my walk-in closet with a massive array of crazy party outfits. Leopard-skin pants, custom platform boots, dozens of hats, sunglasses, wigs, the works. Later, the collection took over the guest bedroom, too (hell, none of my guests were sleeping anyway). When we traveled, fully costumed, people would come up to us in airports and ask us what band we were with. Some small part of me loved the crazy outfits because I could play rockstar, and that somehow excused the drug use.

Mostly, though, the costumes, with hats and sunglasses, were just an opportunity to hide. I didn't fit in with the gays at the club; I just didn't relate to them most of the time. And I certainly didn't fit in with the straight guys. Since I couldn't fit in, I gave up and worked hard to stand out. *Fuck you. I'm not one of you and I don't want to be. I'm a fucking alien.*

Once I had "retired," I found more time to do more drugs. Mostly I was alone during the week, although I wasn't the only "retiree." People would lose their job and come to hang out with me and do my drugs. There was an unwritten contract, at least in my mind: You pretend to like me and I will share my shit. I had devised a kind of "pay to fit in" scheme and it worked well.

On the weekend nights, my friends would arrive around 8 or 9 pm and we would choose our outfits while getting thoroughly coked out. By 11 or 11.30 pm we would make our way to the club and then on to the after-hours club until they closed around 5.30 am. Then we would head back to my place to carry on.

Not long after I had "retired," the party life took a turn. I couldn't seem to make it out to the nightclub. At first, we were missing the club more and more often and would just go to the after-hours club around 3 am for the last couple hours, then one night we showed up and had missed the after-hours club. It was 6 am. We had been so fucked up, so disconnected, that we had missed the night. We had been getting dressed for TEN HOURS. Amped up and thoroughly engrossed in my outfit design, I was trying on my entire closet. At some point, I would need more coke, then more vodka to soften, then another fucking bath to rinse off the sweat, then someone would bang on the bathroom door and I would wake up in cold water, laughing at how close I had come to drowning. Then a ritual toweling off would commence (nothing ruins a pile of cocaine like water), then another snort fest followed by the most pressing question of the century: "What the fuck am I going to wear out tonight?"

More and more often, though, I was too amped, too agitated, too paranoid, too self-conscious to move from my couch. I was stuck. As my paranoia grew, my behavior got more and more strange. I wouldn't leave the condo until nightfall and I would only use the back stairs out of my condo building, darting down the alley like a rat, making a run for it to the liquor store. Eventually, I couldn't leave at all and I started paying a server from a nearby restaurant to bring my vodka, cigarettes, and French fries.

Of course, my new dealer was happy to deliver, sell me stuff, then proceed to do it all with me.

Light to dark doesn't happen immediately and once and for all. As we go from one version of ourselves to the next, it happens one thought, choice, mood shift, action, moment of no choice, habit at a time. Then, all of a sudden, the sun has set. The moon takes over.

CHAPTER 7.
CIRCLING THE DRAIN

At some point, a check I wrote bounced. This had happened regularly since "retiring" from the software firm. When you are blowing (or snorting) your way through big piles of cash at high speed, you don't take the time to sit and fill out the check register balance. I called the number, as usual, to exercise (sell) some more of my shares in order to turn those stock options into nose candy.

"So sorry, sir, those options expired last week. Per the terms of your options agreement, you needed to exercise them within 90 days of your separation from the firm."

"I didn't separate from the firm, I retired."

"I see. Well, you needed to exercise the shares within 90 days or forfeit them."

"I see," and after pausing to select the exact right response, "*FUCK!*"

Click.

I walked into the kitchen and poured myself a vodka tonic without the tonic. I finished it before I made it back to my chair so I had another, then one more just to take the edge off all the coke I had snorted between the first two drinks.

I had forfeited $1,070,000-worth of stock.

Here one moment and then gone, in an instant.

"Well, I guess it's time to sell the BMW," I said to the empty room. And so I did. The next morning, I took some of the money from the sale of the BMW and bought a scrappy little jeep. How fun! Except doing lines of coke in that thing was like trying to sip champagne on a turbulent flight. I barely left the condo at this point anyway. By that night, I had a (really) used jeep, a TON more drugs from the rest of the BMW money, and almost no acknowledgment that I had just lost over a million dollars in an instant. *Things will work out because that's what I'm entitled to – things working out.*

As the endless party wore on, however, patience with my behavior was dwindling. My neighbors were complaining about the incessant noise coming from my condo. Family and friends were getting bizarre calls from me at all hours. I would dial someone I hadn't spoken to in years just to ask the day of the week or to read them a song lyric. But I belonged to this party train and this party train belonged to me. I WAS the in-crowd, finally, as long as the plate was piled high with the good powder.

Without the stock options to cash in, money was getting tight. I had a mortgage on the condo I was living in plus another as investments with my favorite aunt. When I stopped making mortgage payments, she reached out to help. I was unreachable. Over a period of months, I was sliding from "retired millionaire at 28" to full-time coke addict with no job and no prospects. My aunt kept searching for solutions and I kept putting up brick walls. Eventually, she served me with a lawsuit and eviction papers. I couldn't believe she would strike out like this, victimizing her own nephew.

As money tightened, the condo seemed to be less crowded with "friends." It became clear that it was time for me to quit cocaine. I was going to need to take quick action to save my ass. The stuff wasn't working anyway; it just made me pass out or get paranoid. I wasn't getting high anymore. I had one true friend and he stayed with me as I finished what was left of the coke. Standing at my kitchen island, I did a line big enough to end it all, hoping to end it all, and my legs went numb as I passed out. *Please don't let me wake up.*

I want a new drug

Waking up was like crashing down a long flight of stairs, taking out railing and drywall, bouncing to the bottom, and landing in a broken, bloody heap.

Fuck. I'm still here. Now what? The withdrawals were excruciating. It felt like the worst kind of flu, with shakes and chills and bloody nose. I was so sick I could barely choke down my morning vodka.

Dope sick, shaking, shattered without coke, I begged my friend to call the dealer. Sticking to his word to help me quit, he refused, bringing me another vodka instead. I made it for an entire day like this, passing out regularly as alcohol flooded my system without coke to keep me upright. On day two, the phone rang. I don't remember who it was. I lied and told her the party was in full swing. "Hurry, and bring a little coke." She showed up a few hours later. She didn't have any coke, but she had a tiny bit of meth – the "poor man's cocaine."

By the time she arrived, I would have done a line of Drano to feel different. I did a small bump of her modest stash, inhaling with shame. Meth was for face-picking, ID-thieving, bicycle-stealing junkies and I wanted no part of it. It was decidedly low class. *I can't believe I just did meth. Never again. Oh, fucking fireworks. Mother. Fucking. Fireworks. Ka-Fucking-Boom.*

I was alive and whole again. More than whole, I was superhuman. And I could get and stay high for about $20 a day instead of the $200 a day gobbled up by coke. I didn't need more every 20 minutes; that first bump kept me high all day and into the next morning. This was the way! Meth was direct sunlight compared to coke's dim bulbs. Instead of long-drawn-out drunken and coked-out conversations in my darkened living room, meth lit me up. It sent me out the front door and on my way to wreak havoc in the world! Coke is sensual. Meth is carnal.

And out the front door I went. I was evicted from the condo and rented a loft in a seedy part of town across from a massive homeless shelter. By this time, my credit was in the 400s; I had no job or personal references who would vouch for me. But I still had my teeth, which I formed into a smile while I conned my way into renting the place from the unsuspecting landlord. I had no money for rent and no prospects.

My old coke connection called as I was moving my stuff into the new place. I politely declined and tried to let him down gently. "It's not you, it's me. I think it's time we tried other drugs."

A few minutes later, my phone rang again. This time it was my friend Jake, who worked high up in city government. He loved hanging out at my place after the club, doing what I called "baby bumps." He was the type that did a little when he was drunk, but only on the weekends. A hobbyist.

He was calling to ask if I could hook him up with some coke to buy. It was Monday. "Oh, you're a big boy now? You want your own shit?" It's like that moment when a teen moves from stealing their mom's cigarettes to buying their own packs.

"Well, Grant, it was a really fun weekend. I didn't go to work today, I'm out of coke, and I'm starting to come down. I don't want that to happen."

This guy is about to cross the line to the dark side.

By this time, I had witnessed quite a few falls from citizen to degenerate. I wanted to protect him.

My next thought; *Uh-huh! I just figured out how to make some cash.*

With meth as my ally, anything was possible. If he was going to fall, who was I to catch him?

I was uniquely qualified to help with cocaine. I was an expert buyer by this time. I knew how to check for quality, who to call and when, and I was trusted. I had cured myself of the nasty stuff, but some of the more novice party gays needed supply. I brought them $100-worth of the stuff with a smile and without drama. I marked it up to $200 and they happily paid it. They were grateful for my help. And these people were not comfortable meeting drug dealers. I was filling an important middleman niche.

I found drug retailing to be a friendly, gentle little side income. I helped friends find coke, but I wasn't willing to expand into drug dealing. I served a few people and that was all. I was merely a connector, really. But this new part-time job only paid for my growing meth needs. I still needed money for rent. Fast.

Hanging on

Somehow I managed to land a job at the phone company, of all places, in business-to-business sales. It was a fairly long interview process and a very long nine-week training process. I passed the drug screen by giving up the drugs and drinking non-stop for a week before the test. It worked and, since I had quit the meth for a week, I decided this was a good opportunity to quit for good.

I was beginning to see how my current path was leading straight down the drain, and I desperately wanted to feel productive and useful again. The phone job could be my big break back into corporate America. With my leadership skills and résumé, I could rise through the ranks quickly and rebuild my life. For the first time in a long time, I felt a tinge of hope.

Three weeks into the training, I got my first paycheck. It was my first decent bit of income in a while. That afternoon, I reconnected with an old "friend." "Motherfucker, I have money and we need to get fucked up RIGHT NOW. I get off work at 4. Meet me out front." He obliged, and we were up all night. This time, I smoked meth out of a glass pipe. Smoking is more intense than snorting because it hits the central nervous system differently. My body had lost some of its tolerance after four weeks of abstinence and I was intergalactic. I felt too crazy in the morning to show up to training, so I called in sick. I did show up the next day, still up with no sleep, and I remember staring at the lights as I rode the elevator up to my floor, hoping my monster pupils would dilate in time for me to walk past my boss. This blinded me, of course, and I stumbled past the supervisor, but she didn't seem to notice.

For the next several weeks, this party–work–party merry-go-round continued. I somehow made it through training and onto the sales floor, where we took incoming calls from small business clients about their internet and phone lines. The problem with being awake for several days in a row is that you become narcoleptic-like. You can pass out (fall out) at any time. Your body just gives up. One day at work I was on the phone with a client and he was yelling into the phone, "HUH? What the hell are you talking about?" I had fallen out and transitioned mid-sentence into la-la land, where I was speaking gibberish. He woke me up and I heard myself speaking in tongues, then I hung up, praying he wouldn't remember who was helping him.

I knew my time at the phone company was coming to a close. The requirement to show up on time, alert and productive, was just too much for me to manage. I left work early, complaining of a migraine. That night, I decided I would never go back. That night, I decided there was only one job I could maintain. That night, I gave up my amateur status and declared myself a professional drug dealer.

Entrepreneur

The business plan was simple: Serve only the friendly, hobbyist, well-to-do gay party crowd. No coke, no ecstasy, only meth. I packaged the drugs in small quantities and marked them up like crazy. I was clean and presentable enough that neighbors wouldn't raise an eyebrow when I visited my clients in their nice houses and high-rise condo buildings. I was just a friend stopping in to visit. The image was safe. I served a district attorney and their husband, an architect, a real estate appraiser, a banker, a corporate executive, a popular DJ at a Christian radio station, a cop, an elementary school teacher, and even the principal of a very prestigious private school. I specialized in the civilized. It was smiles and hugs and pretty little bags of "crystal." We never said meth. Meth was dangerous. Ms. Crystal was a party.

The raw loft space I had rented downtown was in a neighborhood where I could stay under the radar. The police were too busy with the street crimes and homeless shelter across the street to notice me and my constant visitors. My work happened behind closed doors. The loft provided easy access to my two quickly growing routes, downtown and Capitol Hill, both saturated with my target market – upper-middle-class gays with no interest in buying their drugs from a wholesale drug dealer.

Once a day, I "re-upped" from my dealer, buying enough for the action over the next 24-hour period. Through this connection, I had the best stuff. Total rocket fuel. As a result, I quickly built a thriving business. I had consistent and reliable access and I delivered. I stuffed the packets into the handles of my bike and made my deliveries. Lots of retail dealers befriend their clients, sell to them, then do the drugs with them. Not me. I was all business, preferring to sell as much as possible, in and out quickly, then on to the next delivery.

Safe. Fast. Reliable. I was beginning to get addicted to the rush of the business as much as the drugs.

Then one day, just a few minutes after I left her house with my day's supply, my dealer was raided and she was taken away. One of her workers saw the SWAT van pull up as he was leaving and managed to get away, hiding under a nearby car, watching it all. This was no small affair. We're talking helicopters, SWAT team, the whole nine yards.

"Grant, they came so fast, piling out of the truck, circling the house. They broke through the doors, the windows, all of it. There were guys on the roof even. The helicopter was so low that I could feel the car I was hiding under shaking. They took her away in an ambulance. You know her, she must have fought them hard. Crazy bitch."

I was sad to see my friend and supplier gone. I would have been even more sad if I had known how this would precipitate the rest of my fall. I struggled to find new connections. They didn't trust me, so I had to pay in advance. Since I had no money of my own, this meant convincing my clients to hand over money with the promise that I would return with drugs.

The problem was that my new suppliers were cutting their stuff. In other words, they were diluting the stuff with additives to increase the weight without increasing the meth. When I returned to my customers with the drugs and we discovered it was no good, or only half good, my customers blamed ME for cutting the stuff. Oh, the joys of being the middleman. Now I was in debt to my clients for meth I had failed to deliver. It was a nasty cycle.

I hadn't realized how lucky I had been before with a steady supply of pure goodness. Now there were days when there was no supply to be had. My phone would ring off the hook with demand, all freaked-out addicts looking for more. I was out of it myself, which meant I was crashing. When I crashed, after days and days without sleep, I would be totally out for two to three days. Catatonic.

Tweaked

On one occasion, I was up for several days in a row. About nine hours earlier I'd begun a piece-by-piece dissection of my stereo system. It was to be an art installation of sorts. Stereo deconstructed. I had a vision of how I would rebuild the stereo into a sculpture that would represent a sci-fi communication machine from the future. The floor of my loft was covered with various pieces, laid out with precision, in preparation for the ultimate artistic assemblage.

My leg and back muscles were spasming now from the awkward positions I was holding myself in, frozen, as I gazed with focused scrutiny upon each and every piece I pulled from the wreckage of what had once been a high-end sound system. It might take a minute or an hour to categorize, catalog, and place a particular piece.

My organs ached, desperate for liquid of any sort. I'd even abandoned alcohol by this point. I had given it up long ago, in fact, simply forgetting to drink it. The huge '70s-style amber glass ashtray on the pockmarked hardwood floor was overflowing with several packs' worth of Marlboro Lights, lit at some point and puffed on once, only to be forgotten and discarded, burning down to the filter without further attention. Sometimes the cigarettes tipped and finished burning directly on the floor.

My stomach twisted and tightened and begged for surrender, sharp from the pain of no food. I had long since forgotten to eat. I didn't hear its screams. I was so high that I was forgetting to hit the pipe. This phase, where even maintenance hits are not required for a long time, is known as "orbit," and I had long since left the atmosphere.

My rapt attention was unwavering. I was on a mission, not to be deterred. The loft was connected to my landlord's place. Sometimes he used with me. He had started accepting drugs in exchange for rent more and more frequently as he began a now-familiar slide. Still, I tried to hide the worst of what happened in my place. Typically, I kept music on in the background to squash the tell-tale noises of a tweaker up for days and nights on end in the throes of a drug-induced mania. But my stereo was now a sculpture of the future, so I kept the TV on in the background instead.

I was a 32-year-old grown man in the midst of a multi-day meth binge, sprawled on the floor creating a make-believe communications device that I was starting to believe might actually work. Truth was, I was merely dismantling a stereo and littering it all over my floor. Family, friends, and the outside world didn't cross my mind. I was completely consumed, in the moment, even though the moment was far from lucid. At one point, I glanced up at the TV just in time to see an airliner launching into the World Trade Center. It all seemed like an extension of the make-believe game I was playing. It made sense somehow. So I kept playing, creating an art installation only I would appreciate.

It was September 11, 2001.

Days later, when I emerged from my apartment to make a little money selling some drugs, I was horrified to hear about 9/11 from a customer.

"What the fuck are you talking about? What happened?" I asked.

The poor girl broke into tears, suddenly crushed by the monster burden of being the one to relay the news of the day, and perhaps all that it represented. I couldn't believe my ears. The event on TV had merged with my sci-fi communications device fantasy. I thought it had all been a part of the same hallucination. When I ran out of meth, the device had simply resumed its true shape, merely stereo parts strewn across my apartment, relegated to obstacles between my filthy bedroom and my even filthier kitchen. It was now just a cluttered mess on top of my cluttered mess. I had assumed that the scenes from the TV had also gone back to reality, that the airliner had somehow reversed course and backed out of the WTC.

Fall from grace

My landlord finally got fed up – with everything about me – and insisted on being paid in cash, not drugs. I was three months behind on rent, it was dead winter, and the utilities had been cut off. I convinced a dealer to front me enough to get started again. He gave me an ounce (worth about $1,000). I sold it to my clients.

Soon, they were all calling to complain that the stuff was pure crap. Then my supplier swooped in and stole those clients, blaming me for the quality. It was a hostile takeover of my valuable retail clientele. My clients refused to pay me for the bad drugs and the supplier threatened me with what would happen if I didn't pay up.

No drugs. No money. No heat. No food. Plus a drug dealer looking to collect from me for failing to pay for the bad drugs he fronted me. And "collect" doesn't mean phone calls from a call center. It means a violent encounter.

I was falling fast without the meth.

I abandoned the unheated loft, leaving the only remnant of my prior life behind – my precious mixed poodle, who I adored more than anything in the world. I was leaving my best friend alone in the dark, with no heat or food or water. It broke my heart, and likely his. The landlord was his only hope. I knew I couldn't bring him with me to where I was headed.

CHAPTER 8.
SCRAPING BOTTOM

I was heading straight to hell, but first I stopped off at a friend's place.

I spent about 72 hours crashed on his couch, completely passed out while my body tried desperately to right my wrongs. I rose from the couch a few times to pee and eat chocolate. If you've ever been really sick with a screaming hot fever, you know what it's like to get lost in your body like that. I had no sense of where I was, who I was, when I was. I was "dope sick." My body was revolting: FEED ME METH FEED ME METH FEED ME METH.

Then it happened as it always did, my body snapping to attention once it had recovered enough to hurt, to ache, to beg for more meth. Like a soldier with orders to ship out, I grabbed the single backpack containing my only belongings (one change of clothes, photos from another life, an ID that I no longer identified with, and one dirty, empty glass meth pipe) and headed into the piercing daylight to find more fuel.

A few blocks away, Turner, a frenemy drug dealer, answered my persistent knock. Once inside his apartment, I didn't leave for a month. I found a corner of a walk-in closet to live in, staying quiet and under the radar. I wasn't contributing to the household; I had no connections, no customers, no money, no drugs, no sex to offer, no car. I had long since given up the jeep. In fact, the drugs I bought from the proceeds were gone in three days. One jeep = three days' worth of drugs. I learned quickly that cars are traps for drug dealers anyway. When police are tipped off that you might be a dealer, they don't need a warrant to follow you. Sooner or later, they will find a legitimate reason to pull you over for a traffic violation, or the appearance of one. If your eyes are bulging out of your head as you mumble incoherently and you look like you haven't eaten or slept for years, probable cause to search you and the vehicle is an easy leap to make. Almost everyone I knew that was caught up in the criminal justice system was taken down this way.

I had no currency. I stayed out of the way in the apartment so my uselessness wouldn't be too apparent. They were so busy printing fake checks, IDs, and temporary license plates that no one seemed to notice I was there. At one point, I overheard an important meeting about the organization's car theft goals. "I know some of you have Saturn master keys. None ya fuckin motherfuckers better steal no more fucking Saturns. You stupid fucking tweakers keep getting arrested in 'em. Saturns are for fucking school teachers. You fuckers don't look like school teachers. Honda only from now on. They're fucking easy and we have buyers ready in Mexico."

I had hung around at my old drug dealer's place and overheard the odd conversation about theft, but that crew did simple shoplifting schemes and stole the occasional bike. This crew executed felonies at a much higher rate.

I only left the closet when the apartment was quiet or empty. I snuck spoonfuls of chunky peanut butter I found in the filthy kitchen. I drank bong water from a meth bong left out on a coffee table. One morning as the sun came up, I realized that no one had come back from the night's "errands." Maybe everyone got arrested? I found a bag of meth sitting on the kitchen counter, right next to the peanut butter. I went from "this is not my shit" to "I'm smoking someone else's shit" in three seconds.

I was so high I felt as if I was Velcroed to the ceiling. When the guys got back, it was impossible to hide the fact that I had been using for hours. And it was clear I didn't have anything of my own to smoke.

I'm dead.

These guys had guns stuck in their waistbands. These guys robbed people. And worse.

I'm dead.

These guys were on the run from the law. They were wanted. Badly. For bad things. These guys had nothing to lose.

I'm dead, and that's okay.

But instead of pointing out the missing dope, Turner simply said, "Come on, you're coming with me."

"Where?"

"It's time for you to do some dirt."

And that's how the rent came due.

It ended up being a lot less dramatic than I anticipated.

We got in Turner's stolen truck and drove for 20 minutes without a word. I was still really high and having a tough time sitting, my body twitching and shaking like a bobble head doll. I was engaged in a pretty fierce argument with myself under my rotten breath when we stopped outside a nice little ranch home in a nice enough little neighborhood.

"Get in that jeep and follow me," Turner said, handing me a key.

I did as I was told.

Later, I found out I had taken a rival dealer's car, its side panels packed with meth.

"Don't worry," he said later. "I've got you. You're good with fags and they're good buyers. Help me sell shit to them and you can stay in the apartment."

He paid my phone bill – a lifeline to the buyers. Facebook and other social media hadn't come to the general public quite yet, so the cell phone was everything. We had codes for calls and texts, sure, but anyone could crack those codes in moments. To keep my mom, dad, and sister safe, I had their names in my phone in code as well. But once I had left the loft, I cut my ties to them and vanished from their lives completely. I was breaking my own heart every day and I didn't want to face the truth – that I was breaking their hearts too.

My temporary residence in Turner's apartment helped me get back on my feet business-wise. He hooked me up with a small supply to start, and I gradually rebuilt a little list of customers. I couldn't serve the fancy gays anymore. If I walked into one of their high-end buildings or up their driveways now, the cops were going to be called. I was dirty, with sunken cheeks and dark circles, and I traveled with an odor that preceded me, then lingered long after I had slunk back into the shadows. I was no longer passable as a person. I was junkie trash, and you knew it as soon as you had the misfortune to cross my path. I was shrunken like an old man, turned in on myself, with gravity overpowering me. I was rotting from the inside out. The light in my eyes had disconnected.

If you've ever woken up the day after losing the love of your life realizing it wasn't a nightmare, it was real, then you get it. That was the weight crushing what was left of my heart. I couldn't believe this was real life and no one was showing up to save me. I couldn't just "go home." There was no home.

So I built my new list of customers from the "20" guys. My phone would ring with desperate intensity. "Hey man, can I get a 20?" They would buy $20 bags of meth, daily or a couple of times a day, as soon as they had run whatever scheme they ran to get $20. Many were sign fliers at intersections, petty thieves, prostitutes, while others outright scammed their families for the cash. These were the fancy gays I had been selling to early on, just a few years later in their addictions. It's a quick slide.

Over time, I got fairly adept at couch surfing. I avoided "the apartment" at all costs. The danger and violence there scared me too much. I saw one too many "collections" go very badly. But couch surfing was expensive.

I was smoking about $100 of meth a day, and that was just to stay alive. I rarely got truly high from the stuff anymore. It just made me "right." If I was staying on someone's couch, that would mean I had to feed their habit too. That meant my expenses were $150–200 a day. Since I was buying in small amounts, the margins weren't so good. I had to sell $200 to get $150 worth for me and my couch surf landlord. That's not as simple as it sounds.

If I didn't sell enough to pay for what I was using, I would have to use the part I was supposed to sell. Then I would have to scheme, steal, trick, and cheat my way to putting enough money together to pay back what I owed the dealer. No money, no more drugs. Some dealers would let you ride with that debt, but Turner wasn't so patient. If I didn't return with the money, not only was I cut off from more drugs, but I was also hiding from Turner while trying to come up with the money. And Turner had people looking out for him all over the city.

The other problem, of course, was the using. One time, I got some great stuff. It was on a front (loan), so I owed Turner for it in 12 hours. I camped out in a customer's living room and started breaking up the big bag of stuff into little $20 and $40 bags. With bags and scale out on the coffee table, I was simultaneously measuring and using. Make a bag, do a bag.

An hour into doing this, I was so high I could hardly see straight. I had told customers to come to me, that I was ready with the meth. They were arriving and blowing up my phone to meet. I had been robbed by customers enough times by now that I never gave my actual location, just my general area. The more they called, the more paranoid I got. I was so high I couldn't even bring myself to stand up, let alone to leave the house.

And they kept calling. For hours this went on, and I was moving through the bags, smoking it all and not selling any. Finally, something in me snapped. Insanely angry that the phone would not stop ringing, I answered one of the calls. I gave the guy on the other end of the phone the exact mall shuttle stop to meet up. Then, blinded by uncontrolled rage, I grabbed a baseball bat and stormed through the crowded outdoor mall in the middle of a sunny weekday afternoon. As tourist shoppers gawked in horror, I stood at that stop, pacing with my baseball bat, ready to make sure that he never called me again. I waited, bat in hand.

I was crazed, my head spinning in all directions on the lookout for nearby cops or undercover agents who were likely tailing me, staring down businesspeople who glanced my way in case they were in on this too. Then it hit me – this guy was DEA trying to do a controlled buy. I decided he needed to die. Of course, I was much too low on the food chain for the DEA to care about me, but everyone was DEA or FBI, and every car was packed with people out to rob or kill me. My mind twisted everything to darkness, and logic was swallowed by mania.

In the next moment, the mall shuttle pulled up. The guy saw me standing there with the bat and fortunately didn't get off. I stood frozen, realizing I was about to kill a guy with a baseball bat. When the bus pulled away, I went back to the apartment, turned off my phone, and smoked the rest of the meth.

When I turned my phone back on, it was full of texts from Turner looking for his money and from customers looking to give me money. But I had no drugs, no money, and I hadn't slept. The race was on and the clock was running out. Without drugs, I only had a limited amount of time before I would crash. Crashing meant coming down in one spot for days, so vulnerable to being found by Turner. The only way out was to find the money to pay him back before he found me. The only way to find money without drugs is to steal stuff (I sucked at stealing stuff) or talk customers into fronting money for the promise of drugs (I was a little more gifted at this part).

So I picked up the phone and convinced several customers to front money for "the most epic shit I've ever found but my guy won't front it because it's the best shit ever so you have to give me the money up front if you want any" so I could take that money and pay back Turner.

Sometimes he didn't even care if I paid him back on time, but he'd still threaten me or much worse, just to teach me what would happen if the money was ever late. This time, luckily, he was fucked up himself and feeling no pain, so he was just happy I paid him back at all, even though I was a day and a half late. But high or not, he wasn't stupid. He knew I was spiraling, that I had been up for too long and was about to come down hard, so there was no way he would front me more drugs. He wasn't going to let me pass out somewhere with his drugs on loan.

That left me in a bad place. Turner was paid back with the money I took from six customers. I was sitting back at Turner's shit hole with no debt to him but no drugs, either, and I owed the six customers who wanted their drugs. Who needed their drugs. My phone was blowing up and I was ignoring it. I had dozens of missed calls from one insanely angry junkie client who (rightly) thought I had left with his $40 and wouldn't be returning with his drugs.

Then it happened. The honking started from the alley. Incessant honking. Turner looked at me, glared at me, screaming without a sound. Calling attention to a drug dealer's spot is a suicide mission. You just don't do that if you want to live. Yet this guy was in the alley out back, right under our unit, with his hand on the horn. I was frozen, still hyper-insane.

Turner looked at me. "Are you going to take care of that or am I?"

I knew what it would mean if he took care of it – at the very least, bones would be broken – and I knew this was my fault. Even though I was long past gone, with no shred of decency or honor, I felt some responsibility to protect my customer from his rage. After all, I was the one who created this mess.

So I went out into the alley to save this guy from certain doom. As I stepped out, my customer was mid-stride, halfway between his car and our building. He had almost reached the back gate, gun in hand, with a look on his face that was even crazier than my own.

"I have your stuff," I lied. "Get back in your fucking car and let's go."

And so we did. When we were a block away, I explained the situation, which didn't go so well. He pushed the gun into my side while circling the block like a madman.

"Call him and get my shit, motherfucker. Call him now or you die."

At this moment, gun in my side, car careening around and around a tight city block, I still didn't want to agitate Turner – if I made him deal with this junkie directly, chances are he'd cut me off – but finally, realizing the guy was about to shoot me and seeing I had no choice, I called him.

Turner answered and said, "Sure. Bring him here and I'll give him his $40."

We pulled up in the alley. Turner was calmly waiting and convinced my customer to do a trade. Him for me. The customer released me and pointed his gun at Turner, who quickly persuaded him to lay down his weapon in return for the promise of a "fuck ton of killer shit" waiting inside. I was left in the alley as they walked into the house, quickly followed by several of Turner's more violent colleagues. Yes, I was the fuck-up that took the customer's money and didn't come back with the drugs, but I was Turner's fuck-up, and this guy had pulled a gun on me.

Knowing that the poor guy would be indisposed for a while and likely too battered to drive for the next several weeks, I borrowed the car he had left running in the alley. It was time for me to find a place to hide from the five other guys that were still after me. *No drugs… coming down… must find a safe place to hide while I'm catatonic for a bit.*

Waking up a few days later, I knew immediately that something was wrong. That many things were wrong. First, five guys wanted to find me and hurt me. I had given one of them – the savvier of the bunch and well connected – my backpack as collateral for the money he fronted me; he had known to ask for something to hold onto. He sent me a photo of my backpack. On fire. It held the last remaining signs of my personhood – photos from a previous life, ID, birth certificate, etc. It was now all gone. There was no Grant Muller left.

The other thing that was wrong was, well, more intimate. I had found a refuge, a place to hide, taking advantage of a flirtation I had going with a guy to secure it. I remember taking a swig of GHB (more commonly known as the date rape drug), I remember passing out, and, as I woke up, I knew I had been raped. It wasn't the words I would have used for the experience in the moment, but it was the right set of words.

The words that actually came to me were, "What the fuck, dude? Give me some dope." In my mind, I had prepaid for the dope in bed, after all. He paid up and I smoked the drugs until my hair sizzled. When Mr. Rapey used his bathroom, I snatched his wallet, keys, and bag of meth and slipped out the front door.

It was 1 am. I had a car, some meth, $10 in the wallet, and nowhere to go. I decided the 24-hour tanning salon would be a good stop. I loved the tanning beds because they intensified the high with increased body temperature. It also added some color to superimpose the illusion of a "human being" on my sunken cheekbones and dark circles. A friend rang, checking to see if I had some stuff to sell. "Fuck, yes. What are you looking for?" She told me what she wanted and asked where I would be in 15 minutes. Since she was a friend, I didn't hesitate to tell her where and when to meet me.

Fifteen minutes later, I pulled up and turned the ignition off. Door open and one foot out on the pavement, they lunged at me before I could finish stepping out of the car. The gun that came out of the guy's pocket was almost comical. It was one of those little revolvers designed to fit in a lady's purse. I'd love to say I snickered and said, "What do you think you're gonna do with that little thing?" but I didn't. Guns are scary, even little ones. I gave up the meth without a fight. In no time, they were speeding off with all my drugs. *That bitch set me up. If she only knew what I did to earn them. There are no real friends in this game.*

Surfer boy

Couch surfing had always been an inaccurate way to describe my couch surfing experience. When you are awake for five or six days and then sleep for a day or so, you're not really looking for a place to crash; you're looking for a place to hang out, do lots of dope, and potentially sell drugs. I found the door was always open as long as I had a bag of dope. People would use me for drugs and I would use them for the facilities. It was typically a mutual respect situation. Once in a while, if I didn't like the people, I might steal a laptop or two and trade it in to Turner for meth (laptops at the time were the premium trade-in). And once in a while, if the customer didn't like me, they might pry my backpack off me when I passed out and do the drugs (that I still owed money on). It was a precarious situation.

Once I had been robbed enough, had stolen enough, had burned enough customers and had burned enough dealers, I ran out of credit – and couches. I couldn't seem to get drugs or money. Doors didn't open so easily for me anymore. There was no place to hang out without a bag. On one particular evening, with the snow coming down and the temperature dropping further and further, I tried to sit in a hotel lobby to warm up, but I was kicked out fast. In my mind, I was pulling off the "Oh, I'm just a guest waiting for my friends" pretty well. In truth, I looked like a zombie sitting there. And I'm sure I smelled more like death than life.

For the first time, I came up against the truth: I was homeless and I was on the streets. Literally standing on the street. In the snow.

Without a plan and without the skills to navigate the situation, I started walking. I knew that if I stopped, then I would freeze and die. I kept moving. When my "friend" robbed me, she took my phone and the wallet with the $10 I had on me. Now I was on the streets with a target on my back. Each car that drove by or person that walked past could be one of the five guys that was after me. I had taken their money and never returned.

There was no backup plan. No one was coming to save me. I had brought myself here. I was cold and tired and coming down and desperate. A meth addict popsicle. After a night of walking, the sun came up. The day got warmer, but my blistered feet were killing me. The snow piles melted, forming puddles, and my feet got soaking wet then froze again. I had spent several nights on the street like this before, but something was different this time.

Ready to give in and give up, I ended up on the porch of last resort: a crack house that was infested with desperation, criminality, sickness on all levels, and a high likelihood of a police raid at any minute. But I knew if I stayed on the street, they would find me. I had no choice but to take refuge in this place that, just a week earlier, I had refused to risk entering. I had made them come out to me to buy drugs, and here I was begging for a room at the inn.

But they wouldn't take me. I didn't have drugs and I didn't have money. I had no currency there. Turned away from possibly the last place I wanted to go, I thought of THE LAST PLACE I wanted to go.

"Hey, Mom. It's me. I'm at a payphone in Denver. Can you come and get me?"

"Of course. We're on our way."

CHAPTER 9.
SAVING MY OWN ASS

My mom's house was a complete shock to my altered system. I had forgotten what a house feels like with the heat on and without lines of people waiting outside the bedroom to score drugs. My guest bathroom was stocked with toilet paper and BACKUP toilet paper. It seemed excessive. *Fucking rich people.* I slept for days on a bed, an actual bed. It was like sleeping on clouds. I was up every 12 hours or so for feedings, eating regularly for the first time in years, then right back to sleep.

After several days, I was starting to feel just a bit more like myself, or at least some version of myself from an ancient past. There was a tiny sliver of hope on the horizon. I appeared downstairs and announced that I was ready; it was time to head back to Denver and turn myself into my probation officer. I had been on the run for so long that I wasn't sure what the consequences would be, but I knew I couldn't keep running.

By this time, I had been arrested repeatedly and spent many nights in the county jail. My early stays in jail were terrifying and traumatic. But later on, toward the end of my drug dealing career, it was a place to get food and shelter and network with "colleagues" about the latest in the drug dealing industry – like a business convention for drug pushers. I had been offered probation the first time I was convicted, and, when I failed to stay clean and got arrested again, I spent a longer time in jail. When I was arrested the next time and convicted, I was sentenced to four years in prison. Luckily, the judge released me with "time served" and suspended the prison sentence as long as I didn't violate the terms of my probation again.

As soon as the judge released me, I was gone again, and my probation officer didn't hear from me once in over 6 months. I couldn't go a day without drugs, which meant I would fail a urinalysis test and immediately get sent back to prison to fulfill my suspended sentence, so what was the point of even showing up?

To say my mom was relieved was an understatement. She had recently spent an evening calling around to various morgues looking for me. She happily packed me up in the car, freshly showered and laundered and ready to face the music. Mom dropped me at the courthouse and we knew I would be going to jail for at least a few weeks while they determined the status of my probation and my ultimate sentence. She handed me $20 for the bus ride home once I got out of jail. In my final moments of freedom, I took the longest drags ever on my last cigarette as I watched her drive away, preparing for my stretch in jail.

"What the fuck are you doing right now?" I texted, the moment my mom's car turned the corner and disappeared from sight.

No answer.

"It's Grant. I have $20."

No answer. It was simply muscle memory. I wanted to turn myself in and stop running. I wanted my freedom. I wanted salvation. I wanted to revive what was left of my soul. I wanted to make my family proud again. I wanted that $20 bag more. I can't explain it.

Addiction just means wanting something so badly that we will give up everything for it, even though that something is killing us.

A text appeared on my phone: "Yeah, I got it. Come and get it."

Twenty minutes later I had $20 of meth. I did a tiny bit of it, enough to get me going after a few days without any, and made the rest into two extra light "$20" bags, which I sold to some old customers.

In 12 hours, I had parlayed my profits repeatedly until I had an 8-ball (3.5 grams – worth about $300 at the time) and I was back in business. It's amazing how easy it is to build a profit when you aren't using it faster than you're selling it!

After a week asleep, my tolerance was lower. I was a little high, happy, and cocky from my quick come-up and ready to build up to some real weight to sell again. The problem was I had no supply. I could get smaller bags from the crack house, but I knew I needed to scale up my operation, as my use was going to be scaling up very quickly. If I was going to be on the run and racking up a more serious prison term, I might as well DO THIS THING.

I had converted the 8-ball to cash, shorting bags along the way, and had about $500 ready to invest. *Time to get this catastrophe back into motion.* The peaceful sleep and nourishing food and love at Mom's house was already a distant memory. Probation and prison were completely out of mind... I was completely out of mind.

Word was circulating that I was back online and the switchboards were lighting up. Camped out at the crack house, prospective customers were showing up and no one had any product. I was primed with sleep and food and the drugs were firing me up again after my little break for almost a week! The back of my head was buzzing as if I had been plugged directly into a light socket. It had been so long since I'd enjoyed the invincibility of a novice meth high; the sleep and abstinence had done me good.

I got a call from one of my customers asking me for a hookup and I explained that I couldn't find any. I had just run out and owed almost everyone money, so I couldn't safely call to buy any. If I called Turner, for instance, he would take my money to cover my debt and send me away with no drugs. No supplier was dumb enough to trust me with a front.

This guy wanted a larger pick up and there was some decent money to be made; I could make enough to smoke for a couple of days without a hassle. He mentioned that he had a supplier hookup if I had a car. "Of course I have a car," I replied as I slid some guy's backpack onto my shoulder and walked out the door. I had seen him slip his car keys into one of the pockets before he headed upstairs to enjoy his 20 minutes with one of the crack house girls who hung out to service anyone that had money or drugs to offer.

The car turned out to be a piece of shit. Perfect, I thought. No one calls the police from a crack house to report a stolen piece of shit. I picked up my customer, who was in desperate shape, and we headed to the far west side of town to his source.

"Are you sure this is right?" I asked as we pulled into a neighborhood filled with crooked houses fronted by dirt yards and chain link fences.

"Definitely," he said, and that's when I knew we had some good shit coming our way.

This was one of those neighborhoods in Denver that you don't realize exists unless you know it exists. Denver may be gentle and sweet, but there are pockets of hell and this was one of them.

The dude's house was the last one on the block, backing up to the interstate. Short and narrow, probably 900 square feet, with lots of cars out front. My blood was pumping now. The anticipation of scoring drugs was always a good pre-game high, and when the situation was dangerous, like this, it added a nice shot of adrenaline that focused everything to a very sharp point.

With a quick 1-2-3 knock, we were ushered into the living room and told, "Why don't you sit the fuck down, faggots?" by the woman working the door. I had noticed the camera over the front door and there were several more in the living room. We obeyed and sat on a filthy carpet pockmarked with cigarette burns, since there wasn't a single piece of furniture in sight.

"Get the fuck out of my house," someone bellowed from the back bedroom as a frightened tweaker scampered down the narrow hall and straight out the front door.

And then, "GRANT, GET THE FUCK IN HERE!"

What the fuck? How did this guy know my name? Trembling a little, my friend and I got up to walk back, then…

"ALONE!" the voice boomed from the back room.

The ten steps to the bedroom felt like a thousand as I prepared for certain death. Instead, I got a big happy smile as a welcome. Sitting on the bed with a massive pile of dope was an old "friend" of mine, Storm. We had wreaked some havoc at one point while he was in between prison stays. He was the kind of guy I employed from time to time to convince deadbeat junkies to return stuff they'd stolen from me or pay me what they owed on fronts. Storm was not afraid to bring friends and weapons to get his way.

His pistol was on the bed in front of him, cocked and pointed at a single chair on the other side of the bed. The last I saw him, a couple years back, I had fronted him some stuff. He never returned with my money. As I sat in the chair, uneasy about the gun, he explained that he had gotten "snatched by the pigs" in possession of the stuff I fronted and had just been released after two years in prison.

Storm had renewed his gang membership while in prison. He beat up a rival gang member while in there, got another 18 months added to the original six months for possession, and now he was clearly right back on top. I sat staring in disbelief as he used a huge restaurant-sized ice scooper to make up a bag for me. He offered to front whatever I needed and I was smart enough not to accept more than I had ready buyers for.

I had seen what this guy was capable of and I wouldn't build a big debt with him. I would take a decent amount, though – what I could sell in a night – and double my money, then I'd finally be in a position to maintain a good supply with cash up front. THIS was finally my big break and I was thrilled. He handed me a ready-made bag with these instructions: "Get back here by 3 pm tomorrow and there will be more waiting for you. A shit ton more." Before I left, we smoked a bit from his personal collection and I practically levitated out the bedroom door on the way out.

My customer was waiting for me, looking completely out of place in that dank room, but I was right in place, right where I belonged.

Off I went with my drugs and with my happy current customer grinning from ear to ear because he could see how crazy fucked up I was.

"This shit is out of this world," I said as we got into the stolen car.

We flew back to the crack house. The guy I'd stolen the car from was as angry as you'd expect someone to be who'd finished up with the crack house hooker, gone to grab their backpack and leave, and realized that it had been stolen along with their car... SIX HOURS AGO.

"I'm gonna jack you up for taking my car, man."

All I had to do to get him to calm down was pull out my pipe loaded with big crystals and hand it to him. If there was meth in the pipe, all would be forgiven.

But as we melted the stuff in the pipe, it didn't look right. When we hit it, it didn't taste right. Oh no. My old "friend" had cut the stuff. It was bad. Really bad. I couldn't sell this shit. We smoked about half the contents of the bag, just testing and hoping and waiting to get to the good shit. But the good shit never came.

I called Storm and told him, "I can't sell this shit. It's weak. Bunk."

"You fucking accusing me of cutting that shit?"

"No, no. I'm sure it wasn't you, but something isn't right."

"Motherfucker, sell that shit, come pay me, and I'll make sure the next batch is right. Bring me my fucking money. Don't fuck with me, motherfucker."

I sold what was left of that bad shit to a few unsuspecting people, targeting the buyers who liked to meet up in the streets and alleyways where they couldn't taste test. My plan was to circle back with the good stuff and make up for it later. Right now, I needed the money to pay Storm and save my ass from a painful reprimand. When I got back to Storm's house near the interstate, he welcomed me into the room and laughed as I counted out the bills on his bed, looking down the barrel of the pistol still sitting cocked in front of him.

"Motherfucker, I don't know how you sold that bullshit. You should see what I mixed into it. You are the sales motherfucker of the year."

After all that work selling stocks and bonds, this was my first award in sales, but instead of a special parking spot for a month, I got fronted a bag of some of the best shit I've ever tried.

We sat and smoked some of it together, getting so high that he ended up violent and paranoid. At one point, as I was leaving his house, he insisted I was a cop and made me strip naked to prove I wasn't wired up, then he cocked a pistol and pointed it in my face to get his point across: "Snitches die."

He gave me 24 hours to sell what he'd fronted me.

I ran out the front door, so high and shaken up that I couldn't get on my bicycle. I jogged down the street, wheeling it beside me until my nerves calmed enough for me to ride it. By this time I had been up for several days, long enough for the shadow people to dance in the trees as they threatened to drop out of the sky to kill me, arrest me, or fuck with me long enough to drive me to kill myself.

I made it back to Storm's by the deadline, fighting more intensely with the shadow people than when I left, and richer too. Word gets around quickly when you have great stuff and my phone was ringing relentlessly. I got out of Storm's house, this time without incident and with more to sell – way more. He fronted it again and I held onto the cash that I had made on the last run. Maybe this would be the run when I could roll up enough money to rent a place to stay?

I had "borrowed" a car for this re-up so that I could make a quick delivery to the mountain towns where my old customers were waiting for me. They were ready to supply their little preppy village. The car I was in was allegedly stolen and I had fake temporary tags on – an easy target for any law enforcement, so I had to be careful. At one point I passed out and woke up driving on the grass on the far side of a sidewalk. I was hurtling toward a four way stop, the grass slick and freshly mowed. Luckily my instinct pumped the brakes as if the car was on ice and I stopped JUST inches from hurtling through the busy intersection.

I wasted no time getting out of there, knowing it was likely one of the near-miss victims was calling 911. Once I had put some distance between me and the near catastrophe, I pulled over and poured meth directly into my mouth, a quick way for a wakeup. It wasn't mine to do but I had no choice. After all, it wasn't worth risking passing out on the mountain highway.

With way less in dope than I owed in money at the bottom of that hill, I caught a serious case of the fuck-its. I found some old meth heads to hide out with and we smoked the rest of that shit for a couple of days.

Storm's texts to me became more and more threatening. They were relentless and there was no turning back. He was looking for me and, when he found me, I would be going to the hospital or worse. When you steal from someone in that world, disputes are worked out with violence instead of lawsuits. We hadn't even exhaled the last hit of meth before I was being pushed out of the meth head nest. It was another race against the clock to find a place to hide from Storm before I came down. This come down was going to be brutal. There was nowhere safe to go.

Ready to give in and give up, I ended up back on the porch of last resort – that crack house. I knew it was the least safe place to come down, but I knew that if I stayed on the street, Storm would find me.

Rock bottom

I stepped into that crack house knowing it was the end of the line. The mix of body odor, rotten teeth, and cigarette smoke would have made me throw up if I had eaten anything in the past week. Instead, I gagged like a sick cat. Then I gave up and gave in. I slept for a few days, only rising, or so I'm told, to use the restroom as if sleepwalking before returning to my nest in the corner of a dining room where dining never happened. Out cold. Luckily I had no belongings left to rob.

Later, as I awoke from my daze in the corner, desperate to "get well," which for me could only be delivered via a meth pipe, I was "encouraged" to get my ass up and back to work right away. I had given up, but they weren't going to let me take up space in their house to die. Rent was due for my stay and I had no choice but to work. The pimp-in-residence kept his girls by keeping them strung out and I managed to find $20 bags here and there to keep him in supply. Somehow, there was no moral dilemma in that for me. I was everything I swore I would never be.

It had been a long time since I had kept any promises to myself. I had given up even trying to keep my promises long ago. I was now officially in hiding; I was running from the cops, my probation officer, my customers, Storm, everyone. Disconnected completely from any sense of wrong or right, shame or guilt, hope or faith, I was lying at the bottom of a filthy ocean of despair. The remains of my life had long since decomposed. The bugs had come to get me and shuttle me away, feasting on my death.

Unfortunately, it was not the sweet, true, merciful death that I begged for. It was much worse. My crushed soul and the heart I had broken were shriveled and decayed. Somehow, my wretched body seemed to carry on, no matter what I did to it. Lying there ready to die, I had long ago given up any hope of seeing my family again. I had said goodbye. I was at peace with moving on to whatever hell was waiting for me. Anything different. Please.

But with Storm looking for me I was truly at a dead end. At this point he had made the FBI's Most Wanted list. He had gang members with eyes everywhere and I would not survive a run-in with him. I couldn't live without meth and I couldn't leave to get it. I couldn't run without it. I was weakened and vulnerable in a den of darkness that would sell me out in a heartbeat for just one hit of the pipe. I had been hopeless for years, using against my will, and the drugs weren't working for me anymore. Still, I always pushed on and went to war every day. Somehow I had managed to find new lows.

Twenty-four hours later, I couldn't even get my hands on $20 bags for the pimp. I was going to get thrown out of the house. I was so badly dopesick that I could barely walk, let alone run and hide. It was 28 degrees out.

This day was different and I couldn't find a new low. Or if I could, I knew I wouldn't survive it. I walked two blocks to an all-night diner at about three in the morning and called my mom, begging for her to drive the hour and come and get me. Thank God she did.

I slept for days, same routine as five months before: eat, pee, sleep, repeat. After about four days, I was finally coming around. I went downstairs to see my mom. My sister called and Mom handed me the phone.

She asked how I was and I said, "I feel better. I'm really ready this time. I give up. I'm ready to turn myself in to the police."

"Good," she said, "because they're on their way. Oh, and you should probably know, the suspension of your four-year sentence was revoked yesterday. It might be a long time before we see you. But we love you."

Within ten minutes of that call, I was in a squad car heading to jail.

When I had disappeared into the night a few months back instead of turning myself in, my sister had sprung into action. If they ever had me in their grasp again, she wasn't going to miss the opportunity to save my life.

I believe it's more than mere coincidence that she had a client at work who happened to run a top-tier drug rehab facility in Minnesota. She had told them about her lost brother and they had promised to take me in if I ever resurfaced. My sister was in touch with my probation officer, who had been hopeful there was a small chance I could go to rehab instead of jail. But now, turning myself in literally one day too late, it was looking as if I was on my way to prison for the next four years.

As it turned out, after spending a few weeks in jail as my 36th birthday came and went, I was released into my family's custody. I had a couple of days to wait before my flight to Minnesota, where I would live for at least 28 days instead of going to prison. Vanilla ice cream privilege.

I was completely ready to change my life. I had surrendered, and rehab would be a blessing. I was completely done with meth and alcohol and dealing and life on the streets. During those two days, Mom served as my driver as I directed her around town to shop (on her dime) for rehab outfits.

While out, I managed to hit up a few places to buy some meth precursors (ingredients to cook meth) with my mom's money and stored them in her garage so they would be there for me when I got back from rehab. Yes, I was going to rehab and ready to change my life, but I would still need to figure out a way to get my hands on some shit when I returned. It was my oxygen. You can hold your breath for a bit, but sooner or later you have to breathe again or you perish.

My mom, by court order, watched me get on the plane to Minnesota and I was met at the gate on the other end by some dude that looked way too healthy for my taste. *Must be a cop or a Jesus Freak or both.* I was sober after that flight by virtue of no money, not by, well, my virtue.

I thought about bashing the driver's head in and stealing his car 164 times on the hour-long ride to the clinic. Somehow, once inside and in intake, I surrendered. At that moment, I don't know why, I knew I was done for real. When they weighed me and did their intake check-up, they were clearly disturbed by the look of me and my stats. I was dying. Rotting.

Impatient inpatient

The facility was strictly divided by gender to prevent any rehab sex. Take away an addict's drugs and we will find all kinds of ways to act out. I roomed with two other guys. I don't think they counted on the gays coming to town when they split the camp by gender. A quick gaydar check confirmed my suspicions: I was the only gay in the room and, most likely, in the entire state. Once again, I was separate from, different from, the odd one out. I did not fit.

I deployed my "I may not be tougher than you but I'm crazier than you so don't fuck with me" persona to establish some safety boundaries. I established this persona further during night checks when the nurses would wake me up to take vitals. I was so traumatized from getting robbed and raped while sleeping that I would wake up screaming and swinging. My roommates seemed to get the message, keeping their distance and only interacting with me when absolutely necessary.

The place was very simple – clean and orderly but basic. To me, it was a palace. To have sheets on a bed, a real pillow, a small 1970s oak nightstand, and some sense of safety was incredibly luxurious after the streets and jail and the crack house. And Storm couldn't find me. The food was incredible and all-you-can-eat, so I ate 40 pounds' worth, according to my weight when I left.

I did the rehab work with all my heart. From the moment I entered, I knew it was over – I didn't have to use again. I didn't need to test theories and see if I could drink successfully. I knew I couldn't. We had two 12-step meetings each day and I even went to a 12-step meeting in the basement of a church one night. I just sat there waiting for lightning to strike. And somehow, while I waited, I got the message: "The lie is dead. We do recover."

Twenty-eight days flew by and I learned the lesson that saved my life: I'm not a special addict. I'm not a super-user. I'm not the champion of junkies. I'm simply an addict who doesn't use anymore. For the first time in my life, I had found a place where I belonged. I've earned my seat in recovery. I have a problem with drugs that I want to fix and I understand I can't fix this problem on my own. For that reason, I belong. When I got home to my mom's, as soon as I was able, I declared my freedom by disposing of the meth precursors I had stashed in her garage.

As my sponsor told me, "The war is over when you stop fighting."

CHAPTER 10.
DÉJÀ VU – TRIGGERS

It's been 15 years since I last used alcohol or drugs. The last time was in jail, right before I went to rehab. I crushed and snorted someone else's antipsychotic medication. He hid the pill under his tongue instead of taking it, then he sold it to me for one bologna sandwich. At the time, it didn't even seem like that was "using drugs." I had been clean for about six months before I realized that I needed to adjust my clean date because it turns out that snorting other people's drugs IS using. My sense of reality took years to readjust. I have maintained the same clean date – February 20, 2008 – because I never forget where I came from and because I've had A LOT of help.

After so many years, it seems as if the life I left behind was lived by someone else. It's easy to disconnect from that reality and talk about my past as if it's just a story I tell. It feels like a nightmare that wasn't real. Then it all comes back when I'm driving down that stretch of highway in the mountains, emerging from the tunnel and heading downhill. One minute I'm enjoying the scenery with my husband and the next I'm thinking about how many times I came much too close to dying or, worse, killing someone. Or when I look to the left as I happen to pass THAT neighborhood, hidden unless you know where to look for it. And there's the little squat house where I was strip searched by a murderous psychotic while he jammed his gun into my face. I saw people pay up for drug debts gone wrong there – violent, sickening, traumatic events. Sometimes I tell these stories as I pass by and sometimes I just breathe deep and return to today.

I can't drive through Denver without spotting a place where I used drugs, stole something, got kidnapped, got robbed, or did some sort of shameful misdeed. Yesterday, on my way to run an errand just 20 minutes from my fancy downtown real estate office, I noted all the old spots that hold stories from the "other side." Just two blocks from the office, I sat at the light and watched the crowds congregate in front of our state Capitol. It's an open market for drug deals, for the sale and trade of stolen items and stolen lives. As I sat in my brand-new car with the seat heater on, enjoying the purr of the powerful engine and selling a high-end penthouse on my phone, I felt so distant from that world I had once inhabited.

The light turned green and in just two blocks I was in front of an apartment where I had squatted and sold drugs. On the next block, I spotted a couple of teens who looked as if they were just hanging out, but I know better. I know the signs, I see the details that tell me they're there because they have nowhere else to go. It's too cold to hang out for fun. I hung a left down a long boulevard with a bike path and greenway in between, below street level. I passed the spot where I grabbed someone's bike from them and took off down the ramp, disappearing below before they could catch me.

I passed numerous apartment buildings and condos where I broke into the common areas and tried to steal mail, packages, anything I could find that might be worth something to someone. And just half a mile further, I found myself in the city's high-end shopping district. As I pulled up to the valet, I remembered one particular snatch and grab heist I did with a friend, at the height of our desperation for drugs–food–money–anything. We were on a mission, and I bet I would still be in prison today if someone had tried to get in the way. I shudder as I run into the mall to do some Christmas shopping.

On the way to an appointment recently, I passed our city park, where I've slept, wept, and worse. I passed the 7-Eleven where I was once arrested and released even though I had drugs on me and a warrant; the people I was with were so high priority that the authorities couldn't be bothered that day with a small-time loser like me. A few blocks down, I shuddered with the flood of memories as I passed an apartment building where I was robbed at knifepoint, robbed of money, drugs, and even some of my clothing, but not robbed of my dignity, luckily, which had been abandoned long before.

In the final blocks, I passed the condo building that served as a brothel for an infamous Denver pimp. This was the pimp I sold meth to so that he could keep his girls working for him. And finally I arrived at my appointment in a trendy coffee shop, filled with hipsters. I hopped out of my car and, glancing down as I walked in to meet my client, I realized it's the exact stretch of sidewalk where I shopped for cigarette butts that had some tobacco left to smoke and maybe even some lost change. If only I had known to search for CHANGE. I snap a photo for Instagram.

Last night, I went for dinner – just a quick take-out ten minutes from my house. I was sitting waiting for the curbside service and, looking across the street, I remembered the deal that went terribly wrong there, when I handed over my backpack as collateral with my last few possessions – photos of my life, my glasses, my ID, etc. I remember my desperation and hopelessness at that moment. On the way back home with the food, I passed a mobile home park where I was held against my will for several days, kidnapped because I owed money to some very bad people. I spent days listening to their schemes about some truly horrific and violent crimes. I cringed now thinking about the victims. I cringed now thinking I was part of that violent horror machine. As I turned the corner a few blocks from the house, I passed a gas station advertising meth pipes for sale. Of course, they're advertised as "glass accessories," but I know what that really means. A block from my beautiful home, I passed a couple on foot, and I know why they're walking. They're walking because, if they stop, they will freeze to death and die. Walking with nowhere to go.

The garage door came up and I pulled the car in and walked into my warm house, greeted by the love of my life, and my face grew wet with tears of gratitude. Somehow, the nightmare is over for me. Somehow, I survived the war. But goddamnit, the war hasn't ended. In fact, word from the street is that the war is worsening. Most of my "friends" from combat are now in prison, dead, or have long since moved on to even deadlier drugs. A few made it out, but none made it out unscathed. We carry scars and trauma and disorder with us off the battlefield and bring it back home with us. It's a terrible heavy sickness we bring with us. I know I have seen things no person should ever see.

The line between victim and victimizer is minuscule. I dragged my soul through hell and back in my desperate, selfish search for drugs, and I tore up plenty of souls to do it. My family suffered for years while they were at a loss for how to find me. I became everything I swore I would never be and did all I swore I never would.

This is the broken, weak, soulless creature that I dragged to my first meeting out of rehab. This shell of shame and sickness and self-centered fear was slowly coming alive again after 28 days in Minnesota, but I was very much still on the precipice of another fall into oblivion. I had no faith or trust in any kind of future, but I had a flicker of light, a fragment of hope. Maybe, just maybe, I won't get sent back to the war.

Instead, I regularly lunch with the talented people of Denver who do great work for greater causes. My favorite spot is an upscale restaurant where the city's business and political leaders gather to dream bigger and plan policy that crafts a better world for all of us. When I leave these lunches, inspired by this work, I pass the crack house a block away where I hid, living out my very own rock bottom.

I've put distance between that person and this person by living and serving in recovery. It's a daily commitment of giving and getting help with my disease of addiction. I know with certainty that I cannot survive this disease alone. As we say in recovery, *"I can't, we can."*

The only way up and out is to serve others. I still find myself in rooms, hanging out with drug addicts; they just happen to be addicts that don't use. Finally, I'm at home.

PART THREE: FULFILLMENT

Top of Heart

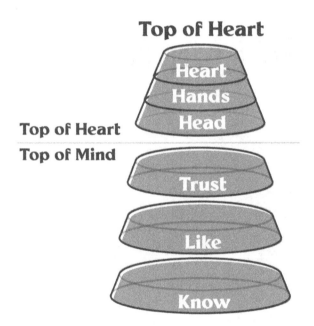

Top of Heart

Top of Mind

CHAPTER 11.
TOP OF MIND

When I returned to the real world after my 28 days in rehab, I was faced with the most basic of decisions. Now what? I was unemployable, flat broke, and emotionally and psychologically stunted. I was, however, riding the "pink cloud" we often refer to in early recovery: the sunrise moment where the most mundane, everyday tasks are magical.

Take away the trauma of homelessness and the desperate race to the bottom in the hell of addiction and it's easy to see why a trip to the 7-Eleven to grab a bag of Cheetos and a Slurpee can be downright exhilarating! The freedom of waking up without the need to "find drugs or die" is palpable. Simple moments in the car without worrying about getting pulled over become magical. I did get pulled over one night, fresh out of rehab, in my stepdad's car. Just months prior, this would have meant an automatic trip to jail without passing go, thanks to my arrest warrants and likely possession of drugs and paraphernalia. This time, the officer did shine his light through my back window (I was so nervous I could hardly speak or breathe and my shaking hands and lack of eye contact must have made me look suspicious), but then he promptly sent me on my way with a warning to use the turn signal.

But still, I had to decide – now what? I was living in my mom's guest room and I was very grateful: I knew I wouldn't stand a chance with this new life if I didn't have a stable living situation with loving and supportive people ready to help me. I had no ID or driver's license, no birth certificate, no passport, no identifying documents at all. Nothing. Luckily, my sister had a car and some free time on a weekday to get me to a church downtown that specializes in helping people like me rebuild their paper trail from scratch.

Privilege alert. I was fresh out of jail and rehab with no identifying documents. I had lost all touch with systems of support, resources, etc. Without my supportive, connected family, I know this re-entry would have likely failed. After all, how far can you get without a safe place to live, something to eat, and ID? I would have simply gone back to the people and places I knew; they would have been my only lifeline. Many friends that are dead, still in prison, or still on the streets bear witness to the alternate path.

A study by the Bureau of Justice Statistics on recidivism among former prisoners over a nine-year follow-up period showed that approximately 68% of prisoners released were rearrested within three years, 79% within six years, and 83% within nine years.[1]

When it came to my former drug of choice, methamphetamine, 61% of users in a random sample of those admitted to a county treatment facility relapsed within the first year after treatment, while 25% of the sample group returned to using at some point between years two and five following discharge.[2]

I am reviewing this discouraging research and reflecting on the reality of substance abuse with a bird's-eye view of it from my downtown office. I can swivel my chair to the left and see the church that helped me rebuild my identity documents. And I can see the alley where I sold meth (and smoked meth) a few times. And there is a girl slumped over and shooting up in our parking lot. It's a popular spot. I've been watching her all day from my office, checking for movement and looking for signs she's overdosing. She screams at me when I get too close. From this view, it's just a couple of blocks' difference between a new life and identity and the old prison of endless misery. Help is just around the corner. At street level, sick and addicted, that perspective is impossible. Those couple of blocks are worlds away.

Starting all over

With fresh credentials, I interviewed for a very entry-level minimum wage phone job warming up cold auto insurance leads. *Wasn't I RUNNING a call center team at Schwab just, like, yesterday? It seems like yesterday.* The work was insanely boring and repetitive, but I over-delivered, giving it my best, and was offered a promotion to supervisor after four weeks. I was thrilled and excited and, for the first time since returning from rehab, I saw a potential path back to some sense of a "normal and productive" life. I agreed to step into the management role, leaving "just the formality" of a background check.

"Uh, well... Here's the thing..." Fresh into my new commitment to live a good and honest life, I gave a good and honest explanation of my situation. The management job offer was withdrawn. I decided then and there that it was time to make my own success, to build a business of some sort that I could accomplish with sweat equity (the only equity I had).

I left the call center and got a server job at Applebee's. After a few months living at my mom's, I had saved up some money for my first apartment. "Apartment" is maybe a bit of an overstatement. It was actually a storage unit; a rather large one, but still a storage unit. I had a mop sink, a hose for a shower, and no hot water, but it was mine. To me, it was a palace, and I was loving living there. The job at Applebee's, however, was not so great. It turns out that I'm a horrendous server. My mind muddled and my short-term memory broken, there were a few too many nacho mix-up catastrophes.

In the past, I had often thought of quitting jobs to become a real estate agent, but I hadn't been willing to exchange my lucrative pay packages for a risky full commission job. Buying and selling a few properties over the years, I had marveled at the mediocre service I got from agents who seemed to be quite well off. I knew I could do better.

While working at Applebee's, I read *The Millionaire Real Estate Agent* by Gary Keller, the founder of Keller Williams, one of the largest US real estate firms. I decided that I could be a real estate agent and quickly build my fortune. I called the local Keller Williams office and begged the managing broker to give me a job doing anything so that I could escape serving tables and learn real estate from the ground up while I studied for my license. It turned out they had an opening for a receptionist. She interviewed me and I felt it had gone well. She seemed quite understanding about my drug possession convictions, but it seemed like forever while I waited to see if they would hire me. Meanwhile, I got fired from Applebee's. In yet another nacho mix-up catastrophe, I took the wrong nachos to the wrong table. This meant that the other nachos would also be going to the wrong table. As my boss yelled at me, I looked her straight in the eye and said, "Get a fucking grip. They're fucking nachos." Needless to say, my serving career was over quickly. Clearly, my street skills were not going to transfer well.

Luckily, after two days of hand-wringing, I got the job at Keller Williams. The pay was $9 per hour working as the office receptionist.

Top of mind

Meanwhile, I devoured *The Millionaire Real Estate Agent* and began plotting my rise to fortune and fame. I figured that the book held all the secrets I would need to make my first million in the next year or so. Two years tops. In this classic bestseller, Gary Keller teaches the importance of gaining *top-of-mind* awareness with people in your "sphere of influence." If people think of you when they think of real estate, or so the wisdom goes, you will get the chance to earn the business. While it didn't hit the lexicon until the early 2000s, top of mind has been around since the '80s.

Think about brands of laundry detergent. Most likely, two or three brands come to mind almost instantly. How about over-the-counter pain relievers? Car brands? Fast-food joints? Advertisers have been pummeling you with brand messaging for years and years to ensure that their particular brands take up space in YOUR brain. When it's time to think about where to eat, you think about the king or the clown or the redhead with pigtails and off you go.

"Think" is a bit of an overstatement. These brands live along the most highly prized boulevard in your brain, right at the top of your mind. We move toward these brands as if by instinct, but it's actually by careful design. Psychologists and neuroscientists are gainfully employed by the world's biggest brands.

Thinking back through my own personal sales experience, this theory made a lot of sense to me. If you were a kid at my elementary school in need of one of those cool STP stickers, I was the first person that came to mind. I owned the STP sticker market. I didn't care about you and you didn't care about me, but that didn't matter – I was STP sticker kid. I had the STP sticker "TOP-OF-MIND AWARENESS."

Later, as a boiler room stockbroker, I called my poor leads five times a day until they bought stock with me. I didn't care about them and they didn't care about me, but that didn't matter. If they needed a stockbroker, they thought of me first. Why? Because I was available to them and called them five times a day, sometimes more. We called and called until they "buy or die!" I was top of mind.

In those stockbroker days, I was fully inspired by the greed hysteria born in the 1980s. Our sales manager had the movie *Wall Street* playing on a loop in the break room. The irony was that none of us needed a movie to make us greedier and none of us were allowed to take breaks from the cold calling anyway. I was living to be Charlie Sheen's character Bud Fox. Charlie Sheen's aggressive sales tactics to get the attention of Gordon Gekko (played by Michael Douglas) were legendary. He called Gekko daily to the point where he basically had a business relationship with Gekko's secretary. He also researched personal and professional details about Gekko's life relentlessly, reading magazine and newspaper articles and consuming whatever other content he could get his hands on about the Wall Street titan.

But what secured Bud's top-of-mind status with Gordon Gekko? He remembered Gekko's birthday and bought him the perfect gift. Bud had read about Gekko's love for a particular Cuban cigar that was illegal to import and proved his willingness to go above and beyond, if necessary.

Bud arrived at Gekko's office on the morning of his birthday, cigars in hand, and refused to leave until the secretary made a face-to-face meeting happen. Because Bud was top of mind for Gekko by this point, Gekko gave him five minutes to wow him. Bud dropped all the details he knew and, even though most of his stock tips to Gekko were worthless, he gave him one particularly great tip. His dad had mentioned a critical piece of breaking news regarding an airline that wasn't public yet. This news would dramatically affect its stock price and – *voilà* – Bud got his foot in the door.

I badly wanted to be the stockbroker in the know, but I didn't have access to any insider information to share with my clients. During those days, the truth is that I didn't get the point of creating a relationship – top of mind or otherwise – with clients. I wanted transactions. The way I saw it, I got paid when my customers bought stock or sold it.

Later, I used top-of-mind awareness to build my career at Schwab. I carefully studied executives, just as Bud Fox studied Gekko, always on the lookout for a way in, a step-up in consciousness, a home in the minds of the ones with the power to change my destiny with a promotion. If you needed to find a potential new manager to promote, I was top of mind. There I was in my Dockers slacks, already dressed the part, with my head down learning the manuals or out in front already leading a team of quote temps. And you probably ran into me a lot in the human resources department (the halls of management), heard from me during town hall meetings, and read about me in the newsletter. I was everywhere. By design. It worked.

Once I was a manager, I didn't stop. I immediately worked toward top-of-mind awareness to ensure I was the first manager to *come to mind* when it was time to promote one of us to senior manager. I remember a trip to HQ for the entire management team (about 65 of us). Who do you think *happened* to be seated right next to the senior vice president on the flight home? I traded a colleague for the seat after hearing the executive's seat assignment, which I learned because I *happened* to be behind her in line at the ticket counter. Creepy? Yes.

We had a lovely conversation on the flight home. *"My car is parked at the airport. Can I offer you a lift home?"* My ambitions to remain top of mind coated the entire executive suite, thick and insistent. When it was time to pick new leaders, the others didn't stand a chance. Who do you think came to mind?!

To be clear, top of mind has its place and can certainly be effective. After all, I did end up getting those promotions. And right up until the time that Bud Fox gave the insider stock tip, top of mind was working well for him, too. We want to be thought of first when they're looking to hire someone, promote someone, buy from someone.

Top of mind is right on target to a point, but top of mind just doesn't complete the circuit of caring. Top of mind answers the question: "When they need x will they think of me first?" But that's not the entire question. The question shouldn't be, "Will they think of me?" Rather, the question should be, "Will they think of me and *will they feel good when they think of me?"*

While I was struggling to launch my real estate career (I shocked myself by passing the real estate licensing exam on the first try) and still working the receptionist job, I was learning top-of-mind tactics. I was working hard to do everything I could to be top of mind as the real estate agent of choice for the entire world (or at least as much of it as possible).

Meanwhile, I was still peeing into a cup for my probation three or four times a week right in front of the clerk; they didn't even trust me to go into a bathroom, pee in a cup, and return without direct supervision. That's right, here I was preparing to be real estate king of the world, but I couldn't be trusted to go to the bathroom alone.

To make sure my pee passed the test and I avoided those four years in prison hanging over my head, I attended 12-step meetings almost every night, where I shared about my using and my recovery progress. Again, though, I left little room for my personality or my humanity. I was top of mind in the meetings. I was showing up and getting to know other people in recovery. You recognized my face and some of my story, but I was skimming the surface without getting real and humble. I wasn't really showing up and allowing real relationships to form.

During the day at work, between calls at the front desk, I obsessed over the idea of top of mind: "How do I get top of mind with as many people as possible to win big as a real estate agent? How do I become the first agent that *comes to mind* the instant that real estate is mentioned or even the tiniest seed of a thought?" One night, I found the answer that I was sure would be my rocket ship to top producer status; in fact, it would make me famous!

CHAPTER 12.
FEAR AND SCARCITY

Before I tell you my plan for becoming THE real estate agent of choice for the entire city, maybe even the entire state, let me catch you up a bit.

After I had closed my first few real estate deals, I was able to move out of the storage unit and rent a little one room cabin in the foothills above Boulder. Later, I was accepted into a prestigious coaching program filled with seven-figure agents and lenders, and I was learning their hardcore strategies for building a hugely successful referral-based real estate practice. It was a little comical hanging out with people who were doing more business in a week than I did all year, but I kept repeating to myself: "You are the combination of the people you spend the most time with."

The coaching was all about high accountability, with two meetings a month where we delivered massive amounts of homework assignments… or got kicked out for non-compliance. It was intense, but I knew that building a business based on these top-of-mind principles would help me get to a place where I could close more deals, just like my coaching colleagues. That was the promise, anyway. I was required to speak with 60 people, attend two events, and have 15 face-to-face meetings *every week*.

We were tasked with developing relationships face to face, one on one. We had to meet these incredibly high quotas to fulfill our homework assignments. I had meetings during breakfast, coffee breaks, lunch, happy hours, networking meetings, and any possible event I could drag my tired body to. There were many days that I had two breakfasts and two lunches! Remember the disaster breakfast I described earlier? I was cramming in so many people that they were no longer people.

I was paying a huge coaching bill every month and running scared from one appointment to the next without uncovering any more business. It seemed the harder I chased people, the faster they ran. There just wasn't enough business available to keep me solvent. I was borrowing money from my family to pay the bills while I waited for deals to close and starting to fear that this was not the right career for me. I wondered if maybe the real estate market was simply oversaturated with agents. I felt like I knew ten for every house for sale. *Maybe there just isn't enough business to support my goals.*

When I brought up my fears about paying the bills, my coaches admonished me for my scarcity mindset and encouraged me to focus on abundance. I was paying $3k a month for their advice. *Why is it that those that have more than me keep telling me I have enough?* They kept telling me, "It's a numbers game. You just have to be in front of a ton of people; you have to be top of mind with as many as possible."

Here I was, in front of a ton of people, asking for referrals all the time, and it didn't seem to be enough. I was like a ghost in constant, exhausted motion. There was nothing left of me, and the numbers weren't improving, at least not at the rate they should have been given my many, many hours with "people."

And that's how I came up with the idea that would make me *top of mind* for the entire city, and maybe even make me famous.

Hitting the airwaves

Radio reaches over 90% of adults. Ninety percent – now THAT is top of mind! I hired the guy who was the master of buying radio time for real estate agents. He was a sure thing! *If 90% of adults are exposed to my marketing, I will be rich and famous.*

And that's how I worked out that radio could be the solution for this haggard, over-networked body and soul. Radio would put me in front of thousands of local people and I could be top of mind with all of them.

We developed a script and found a brilliant DJ with a strong following on a super popular station to endorse me. She loved my approach to serving sellers and she was all in. So was I. My credit cards were maxed as I threw in all my chips for the radio plan, and we ran the spots for four months (I was told that four months was enough time to really see results). I waited for my specially designated phone number to ring. And I waited. And I waited. In the end, the ads produced only two leads, and neither were in any way qualified to sell a house with me. One had a lien against the house that was more than the house was worth and the other was looking to sell their mobile home. What a disappointment.

Here's what I was failing to understand, stuck within the walls of my disappointment. Brands with top-of-mind awareness are the brands that win (and therefore sell more). But at any given moment, unless you're a huge company/household brand name, there is only a small percentage of people ready and eager to buy from you. In light of this, which tactic do you think is more valuable: noticing and temporarily paying attention to this small percentage around the brief period of time they're ready and eager to buy or building a relationship with them the REST of the time?

Many miles of learning away from understanding this concept and still licking my wounds, I took a step back and a good, hard look at the radio ads, the coaching, all the grinding I was doing to get my business to the next level.

I knew that referrals and relationships were the key to getting to the next level. At least that's what my coaches kept telling me. I was showing up, I was meeting people, I was asking for referrals, I was shaking hands and kissing babies! So what was in the way? I hit my head against this wall for a long time. I was taking the actions suggested by the coaching program, so what was the problem?

The *problem* was that I had a secret.

Plastic grant

The secret was me – my dark past, the wreckage I had left behind, the gruesome person I had been for so long. I knew I needed to be accepted in order to sell via relationships. I worried that if anyone truly knew me, they wouldn't accept me, hire me, refer me. Now, belonging wasn't just an urgent human need, it was a requirement for my success and livelihood.

My solution was to create the persona of "Grant Muller – the Real Estate Agent," the kind of agent any buyer or seller would want to hire. I stepped into this role with vigor. I worked non-stop and crafted an identity around an unflinching ability to get the best deal and outwork anyone anywhere. This was not a false narrative, just a little one-sided and exaggerated. I left no room for personality or humanity. And it worked – to a point.

The problem was that, when I did have sales, it felt empty. I couldn't truly live those exciting wins with my clients because I wasn't truly there. "Grant Muller – the Real Estate Agent" would cash the checks, but it was merely transactional. My happy clients would invite me to dinner to celebrate and I would turn them down. Carrying "Grant Muller – the Real Estate Agent" on my shoulders for the length of a meal was too exhausting.

Top-of-mind selling is all about this half-formed approach: showing up as the most likely person to gain acceptance, to belong, to be chosen for the sale, the job, the promotion. It can work, but only if you are willing to survive by constantly replenishing your list. Top-of-mind clients rarely refer their friends to you, and they're loyal only until something better comes along.

I was finding out that my connections were weak and vulnerable. I was top of mind with my clients until I wasn't, and it was easy for the next agent to take that spot in my client's mind. If I wasn't the last postcard or email or call they received, my position "at the top" of their mind was tenuous.

Top-of-mind selling, with a true know–like–trust relationship, is a great place to start, but it typically works more like this Messenger interaction I had just the other day:

Facebook friend request.

24 hours later on Messenger:

"Hey man, how are you?"

"Fine, thanks."

"May I ask you a quick question?"

"Yes?"

"At this time neither is probably keeping you up at night but are you more worried about your wealth or your health?"

Sensing a set-up, I reply, "Why do you ask?"

"Well, let me cut to the chase. Are you familiar with ketones... supplements... mention of a video..."

"May I ask YOU a question?"

"Okay."

"Does this sales strategy actually work for you? You know, send a friend request to someone and then go in for the sale 24 hours later?"

"Yes it does because most people aren't so closed-minded."

Unfriend. Block.

I knew I couldn't keep up the pace of being everything to everyone, hoping they would buy from me. I could only meet so many people a week and keep it all straight. There had to be a better way. I was running around like crazy and I wasn't closing any more deals. In fact, my business was declining in spite of all my efforts (and my investments in coaching, radio, and internet leads).

I took a long, hard look at my business. I checked my activities and focus. I looked at all the deals I had closed in the past 12 months. I realized that over 90% came from past clients and their referrals, not from all the people I was "in front of." Rather, the referrals came from my true connections, my real relationships. My referrals came from my core set of allies who wanted to see me succeed, not the random strangers I exchanged cards with at networking events.

I realized then that I had to stop playing at relationships — being in front of a lot of people and staying top of mind. I had to dig deeper and build meaningful relationships if I was going to make it in real estate.

I had to get real to make it

Meanwhile, I wasn't fully showing up in my recovery relationships either. I dutifully attended 12-step meetings and began to build core friendships for the first time in a long time, but when I shared my story and spoke up at meetings, I held back. I presented myself as the bigger dealer, the badder doer, the sicker soul. In recovery, we call that "junky pride." As sad as it is, I wanted to present myself as sicker than I was not only to make sure I belonged but also to make sure I belonged in a front row seat. My sponsor called me out for this junky pride and lack of humility and truth, warning me that I wouldn't stay clean if I didn't get real, but I ignored his warnings.

And then it happened, that one dark moment. Alone in the cabin in the hills, I heard that voice so many of us in recovery experience.

What's the point? Why does all this matter anyway? Why did I get clean? I'm still poor, alone, miserable. My prospects are bleak; my probation seems never-ending. I might as well just find the relief that is easy and full and right. Just a drink or two, maybe some meth or coke or whatever. Maybe I belong with oblivion.

I reached for my phone as we are taught to do in recovery when relapse is looming. I scrolled through names and numbers I had dutifully collected at meetings. None of them truly knew me, or what was going on with me, or what a mess I was. How could they? I wasn't sharing in meetings who I really was, how terrified I felt. I had a decision to make right then, in the lonely darkness of that cabin: return to my life on the streets or get real with someone. Anyone. Let them see the truth I have hidden even from myself.

I had to get real to survive.

CHAPTER 13.

GET REAL

Unfortunately, my conscious desire for survival was being attacked by the disease of addiction[3] that was trying to kill me.

My disease was tugging at me to return to the streets. My disease sent me mental memes of euphoric recall. My disease suppressed the memories of all the shame, degradation, and utter desperation that had brought me to my knees. My disease promised it would be different this time around; I could hold onto employment and just get high on the weekends, with no need to get back into the dealing game.

I could use meth like a gentleman.

My disease told me that my downfall was inevitable, so why wait for it? Why not take action now and jump into the splendor of those spine-tingling episodes of ecstasy? Surely the best of highs would be waiting for me, given my low tolerance levels after months of abstinence. Oh, the hits would be epic and the rush would last forever.

My disease reminded me that I'm not worthy of a good life, and no one else cares about me. My disease kissed me on the cheek, got down on bended knee, and promised it would never hurt me again. My disease promised it would all be different this time.

Unbeknownst to me, my disease was speaking a different language. It was living by different priorities. In essence, my disease was the Cookie Monster on *Sesame Street*, except instead of cookies, it craved brain matter, starting with the white matter that allows us to learn, make choices, adapt to new situations, and receive information. A 2002 psychiatric study[4] showed that, in the brains of cocaine addicts, the normal, age-correlated growth of white matter is nonexistent. In addition, white matter's cousin, gray matter, which helps regulate emotional impulses and rational decisions ("Hello!"), was also falling victim to my mental Cookie Monster and being eaten away.

Even so, I had been in love with my disease for close to a decade. It was an incredibly abusive relationship, but it was all I knew anymore. I had escaped in the night, skipped town, left without a note. But I was lonely and empty now, and I missed my sickened existence, the trauma I had come to depend on, the anger and fear and drive to get more-more-more that was my never-ending internal machination. The rush that comes with living on the edge of death is perversely life-giving. And I missed my friends from the old "neighborhood," the ones I stole from and the ones that stole from me, the liars, the thieves, and the whores that were my colleagues in filthy distress.

Sitting in that cabin, I felt the pull to all of this, the inevitable gravity of a hellish momentum I had created over too many wasted years. The compelling inertia was heavy and dark. I wanted to pick up a meth pipe more than I wanted love, family, life, breath. As I sat there fantasizing about what my first hit would be like, the blood drained from my head. I could feel the drop like a ten-story free fall in my gut, as if my insides were unraveling back to my one and only love, my sick love, my deadly love, but my love.

I decided to go back home, return to my captor, beg my abuser for forgiveness for running away. There was nothing here for me anyway. *I must smoke meth again. It's simply what is meant to be.*

But not until tomorrow.

In perhaps the smartest move I had made in a decade, I chose to wait until the next day. Just for now, I would sit on my hands, taking a wise suggestion I had heard in the 12-step meetings. I would handcuff myself to this moment. I would use drugs again, sure, just not right now. It was a life-changing, life-saving procrastination.

It was a long night with no sleep, laying there as if I was waiting for an attack, waiting to get stolen in the darkness. As light forced its way through the tiny cracks in the rickety frame of the cabin the next morning, I jumped up to get dressed for my job, remembering the night before as if it had been a dream. Somehow, the pull wasn't so strong now, and I remembered the beatings that would be waiting for me if I returned to my old life, if I gave myself back to meth.

Dashing out late to my appointments, buttoning up my thrift store shirt on the go, I thanked God for saving me from myself that night. I made a promise prayer: "Dear Lord, God, Higher Power, Dude in Thine Clouds, Whatever or Whoever You May Be, I renew my vow to do whatever it takes to stay clean, in this moment. I am willing. I surrender to the program of recovery, to the truth of who I am, and to the work that lies before me. I will dive into this work as if my life depends on it because, of course, it does. If I don't get better, it won't get better for me."

At a 12-step meeting that night, I opened my mouth to share about my very close call. But first, I bragged about all the drugs I could find quickly, and in high quantities, if I chose to, with my big-time hookups. My sharing was full of that junky pride. What a great addict I was! What an extra bad addict. This was my typical share, campaigning for my position in the addict hall of fame. But this time I stopped myself mid-sentence, tears searing my cheeks.

"Goddamnit, that's bullshit. I burned all my connections. I wasn't big time, not that it matters. I was a street-level punk with no street smarts. If I don't get real now, I'm not going to make it. If I don't get fully honest, I'm a dead man.

"I'm fucking scared; I almost gave up last night. I can't believe, after years of being homeless, facing down years in prison, after rehab and all these months, I could come that close to giving it all up. I'm fucking scared because there is no question – one taste and it will all be over for me. I can't go back there; I will not make it back alive if I do."

The heat in me was rising as I spewed forth, half talking and half gulping for air while blubbering.

"I'm fucking scared because I know, without a doubt, that one taste will make me useless against my disease. It will get me alone, separate me from all that is good in me, and kill me, and it will be a long, slow, painful death. I'm fucking scared because I don't have enough strength to fight this thing that wants to kill me. My willpower is not enough. I know that, if I use again, it will be like jumping back into the path of the tornado. No willpower can stop a tornado. This thing is so much greater than I am. Please, fucking help me!"

In that moment, I was revealing my true self for the first time in these meetings, getting real with myself finally, vomiting tears now in front of 25 addicts, who, far from shocked, mostly nodded with a knowing look. I realized that I was ready to surrender for real this time. I needed them. I needed a power greater than myself to fight this thing. It was time to surrender to what is real about me as if my life depended on it – because my life depended on it.

The only chance I had at a new life, the only chance I had at freedom, the only chance I had to survive required me to abandon all pretense. No more lies, half-truths, bullshit stories. I needed these people if I was going to make it. I knew I needed to somehow become a part of this group rather than apart from this group.

I had never been a joiner; I was always the outsider. But, just like in the wilds of Africa back home, diseased outsiders get picked off easily. I needed to plant myself in the middle of the herd and depend on their better thinking to carry me through.

I had been trying my whole life to fit in, belong, find my people. But whenever my people found me, whenever they welcomed me, I resisted. Were they welcoming me or the bullshit character I had crafted to fit in? How could I belong with them if I couldn't even belong with myself?

These recovery meetings were filled with the craziest variety of human beings, but they all had one thing in common: They had all been to hell and returned badly beaten, inside and out. Each hell was a bespoke kingdom of despair filled with each person's personal fears and darkest demonic pits of misery.

It was a stark choice – belong or die. Luckily, for the first time, I truly belonged.

I began the work of the 12 steps. Meetings are great, but I was promised that change would come from the step work. We worked out of a workbook and I wrote answers to 60+ questions for the first step. Then I met with my sponsor and shared all my answers. Somehow, he wasn't shocked, only accepting. Then we moved on to the next step. The more I wrote, the more I came to see myself as I really was for the first time in my life.

Much of what I saw was repulsive. I was facing the truth about my worst actions, seeing the truth of what I had put my family through, seeing how I had contributed to so many people's addictions by dealing to them, and seeing my most shameful actions in the light of the day, out in the open. It hurt like hell and it healed, too. As I got real with my sponsor, I started to change. Later, I would learn what therapists know: When we are seen and accepted as we truly are, this is when change happens.

Over the next few meetings, I kept showing up and telling my real story. It was time for me to look for ways to reveal my humanity instead of my superiority. I let the raw pain, the burning truth, the sickening shame work its way from deep within me and out of my mouth into the room. The grief and shock and dismay from years of morally bankrupt, truly repugnant behavior seemed as if it would destroy me as it left me. It was poison passing through me and it felt like barbed wire reversing course through my insides, shredding me as it extricated itself.

For the first time in my entire life, I had shown up as I really am. It was the first time I had truly seen *me*, and certainly the first time in a long time another person had truly seen me. In that incredible moment of compassion and love, my sponsor's acceptance of me as I really am brought me home, where I belong. For the first time ever, I was really home. I could put my bags down and unpack. I belonged.

I had awoken and been changed in the deepest ways. I had taken full ownership of, and at the same time been relieved from, the weight of my countless wrongs. Belonging, joining, becoming a part of that which is greater than myself means sharing that weight and tapping into a power, an intelligence, a love much greater than I ever had access to before. That is what it means to belong. In recovery we say, "I can't, we can." I was starting to see that.

I was lighter, gentler, softer, and much stronger. Being seen as you truly are and loved anyway is powerful. And seeing yourself as you truly are and loving yourself anyway is a gift. That smooth, sure, unflinching love emboldened me to move through the world with a quiet confidence, a bold and brave approach, an open heart. My vision had shifted 45 degrees.

On another dark night in that cabin, I was sleepless again. This time, it was excitement keeping me up. For the first time in ages, I could see a better life unfolding. I felt like a member of the human race for the first time, I felt closer to my higher power, I felt hopeful. I saw endless possibilities, the greatest love and joy, and my own infinite potential.

Maybe this was the spiritual awakening I keep reading about in the 12-step recovery pamphlets.

CHAPTER 14.
LIGHTNING STRIKES

The next morning in the real estate office, I strode through the glass doors with a fresh set of eyes and a different heart. I was an astronaut returning to Earth from a moonshot, an astronaut who was being ushered directly from the spaceship into a sales meeting. As I landed from my other-worldly awakening, hearing people discuss the weather and other mundane topics as they filed into the conference room seemed trivial to say the least. The conference room itself seemed even more beige, and the coffee was weaker. The hellos and smiles and hugs were saccharin.

I was in my own skin for the first time, and I realized I wasn't the only one playing along in real estate land to fit in. For the first time, I noticed the forced smiles and the overplayed exuberance about a weekly sales meeting. And here I felt suddenly like an alien again, landing with the truth of who I am, surrounded by those clearly living the vision of what we would imagine a real estate agent to be and look like. You know – careful hair, thoughtful outfits, smiles just so.

Our sales meeting began with the typical agent banter – lots of posturing about who got what deal under contract, who won which listing, who was having the best month ever. All the usual transaction brags. Our guest speaker launched into our training. The idea here was that we reached out to our clients in various ways a ton of times each year (30+) so that we would remain top of mind as a real estate agent. That way, the idea goes, we would be the first to come to mind when they needed help to buy or sell a house. Hence, "top of mind."

Thirty or more times a year is about three times a month. You might send a postcard bragging about your recent sales once a month, send an email newsletter once a month (bragging again about your sales and ultimate unquestionable superb superstar status as a "top producer"), then call them once a month to see if they have any referrals for you. That would be three "touches" for the month. When learning this client touch process, I often had the thought: "If someone reached out to me three times a month in this way, they would certainly be top of my mind... as a pain in the ass!"

As it turns out, I would soon learn, I wasn't alone. Every non-sociopath agent out there is terrified of being "that guy" – the dreaded telephone bloodhound, clamping onto people's ankles and refusing to let go. Every agent – hell, everyone in sales! – is looking for permission to stop doing that. For years, they have been waiting for someone to offer them a better way.

For now, though, I felt I had no choice but to go through the motions of becoming a three-times-a-month top-of-mind pain in the ass. Today's lesson was focused on how to make the monthly call. After all, what do you say? It's slightly – okay, insanely – awkward to call someone out of the blue for a catch-up and then somehow work up the nerve to ask for referrals. But the trainer had a plan for this and I was all ears, ready to learn the secret to the magic referral-generating phone call. The secret, we were taught, was to call the person and follow a script known as "FORD."

You call up and ask, "How's the **F**amily–**O**ccupation–**R**ecreation–**D**reams?" But you don't do it all at once, he said. You let them chat about how their family is, then ask casually, "And how are things at work (occupation)?", "Do you guys have anything fun planned for the summer (recreation)?", "What goals are you working toward (dreams)?" Then comes the kicker. At the end of the call, be sure to ask, "By the way, who do you know that might be looking to buy or sell a house in the next 90 days?" Or you might say, "You know, interest rates are low and the market is getting better, would you like a market evaluation for your house and we can see if you could move up to a bigger house?"

Wait, what?! That's the magic call? I have to pretend to shoot the shit with some poor person and then nail them at the end by panhandling for a referral? This fake-friend-so-you-can-get-a-referral stuff was making me violently ill. My chorizo and green chili breakfast burrito was about to re-enter the atmosphere with force. I had to get out of that conference room or things were going to get ugly. Surely I hadn't returned from hell to live THIS life? Surely I hadn't just gotten real for the first time in my adult life so that I could manipulate people into thinking I cared about them to sell more houses? I was more honest with my clients when I was a drug dealer!

Panting through a series of cigarettes in the underground parking lot, I tried to make sense of the training. I stared at the red Audi convertible driven by my sales hero in the office. It was my dream car. I wanted this success so badly. *Is this fake phone conversation stuff the only way to make it? I like the concept of FORD to help ease the conversation, but that ending just ruins it all.*

How on earth could I be okay with pretending to care about someone for the sake of taking from them? I had finally escaped that mode of take-take-take and here it was again, just in a sanitized, legal, business-approved format.

I wanted to succeed at real estate sales so badly. This was my opportunity to restart my life and rebuild my momentum toward something meaningful. I had to make a go of this solid citizen thing because being a sick addict dying on the streets was not looking like a great alternative. Sell houses or sell drugs and die – that's how I saw this fork in the road.

I wanted to prove to myself that I could still love business as I used to. I needed to prove to myself that there was a mission here worth capturing. I remembered the rush I got from solving business problems back in the day. Now, I hoped it would ease my withdrawal from the rush of the drug dealing game. I needed to feel useful and significant. Was real estate success going to require that I run around pretend friending everyone that might have a house to sell?

No wonder people hate selling as much as they hate salespeople! Who wants a career like that? I drove up the long, winding road to the cabin in the hills disappointed and dejected. I knew I couldn't go back to being a faker and a taker. I knew getting real was the key to my freedom and salvation. I actually thought about quitting real estate. I just wasn't willing to sacrifice the character I was rebuilding for the sake of money. Maybe it was time to find a different career path.

But I was unemployable. No one was going to hire an absolute failure with years of blank résumé and a criminal record in the middle of the great recession.

The only real choice was self-employment because I was the only one dumb enough to hire me. A real estate career allowed me to be self-employed without a huge cash investment. No one was going to lend me money, not even for a pack of smokes. This had to work. I had to make it or it was back to the streets, and I knew that meant dying a slow, painful, lonely death.

I fell asleep reading my worn and heavily highlighted copy of *The Millionaire Real Estate Agent*. This was my bible of real estate success, the book that brought top-of-mind strategies to real estate agents around the world. This was the book that had laid out a path to real estate millions, built from the study of dozens of millionaire agents. They were all my role models in real estate, and they were all incredibly more successful than I could imagine. But as I read some of their stories again, I saw through some of their manipulation techniques and self-centered approaches. They seemed to be great people following a flawed philosophy.

But who was I, flat broke with very few real estate sales compared to them, to question their wisdom?

Breaking through

I woke up in the middle of the night with a jolt. The cabin was dark and silent. I lay still, hoping to go back to sleep, but it was no use. I just couldn't. My head was spinning, racing. I hopped out of bed and scribbled on a sticky note, "Relationships that transcend transactions." I stared at the four words, trying to decode them as if someone else had written them. I gave up and got back into bed, wondering if maybe I should get into the car, drive to Denver, and just get on with the inevitable relapse. Luckily I fell asleep before I got the nerve to go. Another lucky reprieve from madness.

The next morning, I found the sticky note attached to my thrift store coffee mug. What if I could build real relationships that transcend transactions? How about relationships built on true heart-driven human connections rather than self-centered manipulations? Maybe top-of-mind strategies such as staying in touch and adding value on a regular basis are okay, just not enough.

Maybe top of mind is just the beginning, but what I'm really craving is more. I do have a thing about more after all. What if there is a next step, a place where we can get real, come from the heart, build meaningful relationships, and set our own agenda aside? What if we can leave all the sales tricks and fake scripts and dialogues behind and reach for what is honest and right and the best in all of us? What if I follow my heart instead of my mind?

For the first time, I saw that what had saved my life in recovery – getting real, uncovering truth, letting go of self-centered fear, building meaning and purpose, belonging – could also save my sales career. I spent all day bouncing through scenarios, considering the implications of this new approach, imagining the possibilities. I continued late into the night. The last time I had stayed up like this I was high as hell, channelling destructive forces for evil means. On this night, I was racing toward all that is hopeful, loving, inspired, and aspirational. It wasn't just time for a new sales process or marketing method; this new life would require an entirely different worldview... a move from top of mind to *Top of Heart.*

Top of Heart

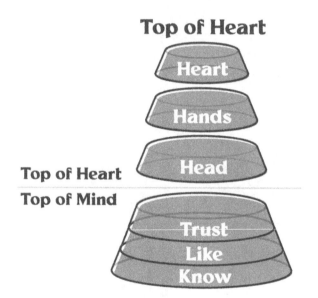

Top of Heart

Top of Mind

CHAPTER 15.
WHAT IS TOP OF HEART?

My life's journey has taken me to hell and back in search of belonging. At a fundamental level, we all seek to belong. In our individual quests to become a part of the human race, we often lose what makes us unique and special. We confuse acceptance with sameness and fitting in with belonging. We round our sharp edges, tone down our colors, and soften our voices. We confuse what is popular with what is true. We confuse common with beautiful. We busy ourselves with "adult" work, mainly making sure we don't stand out. We follow the rules, do what is expected of us, and keep relationships safe, secure, and sufficiently superficial.

This is certainly the case with most business and sales relationships. Top-of-mind tactics keep us "in front of" rather than "with" people, teaching us to stay relevant rather than real. But the age of putting up a business front is over. Going through the motions, playing "numbers games," and referring to potential human relationships as "prospects" and "leads" is no longer cutting it.

We're in an age where automation is replacing more and more of the moving parts of sales transactions. According to the McKinsey Global Institute,[5] one third of sales and/or sales operations tasks can be easily automated with current technology.

Artificial intelligence (AI) is learning faster than human intelligence ever could. There is simply no way to keep up with a machine that can grow through many generations for each of our human generations. Knowledge is already a commodity. Clients no longer follow me to the next house during showings; they simply look up the address on their phone and I end up following THEM!

And this is just the start.

Once this transformation is complete, all that will be left is our ability to forge real human connections (and ALL the things that come from those connections), something that automation cannot replace, at least not for a while. AI can respond incredibly accurately based on the right inputs, but it will be a very long time before AI can "read between the lines" or notice subtle shifts in facial expressions and other non-verbal cues. And we are much more than inputs. The heart and soul of our human experience will be the very last piece for AI to conquer. In the meantime, AI is a tool to manage the least human tasks, freeing us to manage the most human ones.

Old-school (and still prevalent) sales strategies are fake and tactics driven. They go AGAINST our natural human instincts, which is why they so often feel bad and fail. People in business and sales feel as if it's the only option, so they keep forcing it. And whether it works a lot, a little, or not at all, they remain in the cycle. As a result, people feel that, no matter how wrong it feels, "it's worth it" to think and operate that way. You can spot these sales methods in play when churn is high, loyalty is low, and lifetime value of customers is a failing measure.

"I'm sure your girlfriend would feel special and loved if you went the extra mile by upgrading to the diamond setting."

The salesperson was appealing to my friend Seth's ego and desire to make his girlfriend happy during a recent trip to purchase her a bracelet. She had already indicated exactly which piece she wanted, and Seth had been saving for months. He told me he had felt diminished, emasculated even, by the salesperson, as he insisted on buying the "lesser" bracelet. With that one sentence, the salesperson had extinguished the flame of excitement my friend had been stoking for months in anticipation of this loving gesture.

"I couldn't help but wonder in the back of my mind if Jackie would be disappointed. Was she just pretending to want that bracelet while secretly hoping for the one with the diamond setting? I didn't think so, but now the seed of doubt had been planted."

That sales jerk ruined the entire experience for Seth.

Seth won't be returning to that store any time soon. They lost future sales and possibly risked a negative review that would affect their sales to others, not because they dutifully attempted the upsell but because they failed to simply listen to and consider the human being in front of them.

According to the National Association of REALTORS®, 68% of sellers who used a real estate agent found their agents through a friendly referral (friend, neighbor, relative), 53% used the agent they previously used to buy or sell their home, and 90% of sellers would "definitely" use the same agent again to buy or sell their home.[6] Yet the typical real estate agent earned only 16% of their business via repeat customers and 20% through referrals from past clients.[7] In other words, sellers say they would use their previous agent again, but they rarely do.

It doesn't have to be that way. Being a salesperson can (and should) be a natural outgrowth of love and compassion. Top of mind ignores this fundamental principle and forces people to suppress those instincts in an effort to avoid "blowing the sales" via a misstep. How do we build on top of mind and take the next step? Where do we go from here?

With the Top of Heart worldview, we get permission to bring our true selves into every business process – sales, service, leadership. Business relationships are not separate from personal relationships. Top of Heart is about relearning what human nature already knows: Business relationships come from the heart, not the head. We stop swimming against the tide. We bring the art of persuasion back to square one and relearn what our hearts never forgot. We prove that sales and human relationships are not contradictory notions.

If the jewelry sales rep had taken some time to have a conversation with Seth, they could have learned important details about the purchase. They could have heard about Jackie's specific wish for that EXACT bracelet. They could have heard about Seth's months of diligent overtime to save for it. They could have celebrated the moment with Seth, become a part of this important memory, and perhaps even gained a customer for life.

As I worked the 12 steps as if my life depended on it (because my life DID depend on it), I began to unearth some old relics of my prior personality. I found an odd sense of humor, bucketfuls of sensitivity, and behavior more outgoing than you would expect from an introvert. There were some newly developed pieces of me as well. Many were problematic, such as extreme selfishness and a talent for rationalizing the most abhorrent behaviors, for instance. But there was some stuff I wanted to hold onto. I had learned a toughness and developed a survival mechanism on the streets that continue to serve me (and others) to this day.

As I learned to live with a Top of Heart worldview, I learned to bring all of myself to my work. I was getting real for the first time because I had no choice. Recovery requires an ongoing and rigorous self-assessment. As I learned to be myself, I brought more value to my colleagues, clients, and fellow recovering addicts. Work and play just became life. Congruency, it turns out, is attractive to clients and friends alike. Work became way more profitable and life became way more fun.

Top of Heart doesn't discard top of mind; it builds on it. The top-of-mind framework, the know–like–trust made famous by so many sales and marketing trainers, is where we begin. It's the foundation I started with in my real estate practice. I shook hands and kissed babies and got *in front of* as many people as possible. Remember the awkward breakfast? It was a mess, for sure, but that vigorous networking activity did help me get my business off the ground. Let's explore why.

Revisiting top of mind

Know

In order for a buyer to work with us, they must know we exist. Whether we're selling a bag of potato chips or a life insurance policy, they must think of us first as soon as their own personal sales cycle begins. It goes something like this:

Let's imagine you've decided to move out of state to be closer to your family. You're tired of the big city, and it's time to move back to the small town where your parents and siblings still live. You look up your house value on one of the real estate websites, then you check another, and another. By now, you have three wildly different values. You're already confused and uncertain about what price your house will sell for. To buy your dream farm in your hometown, you know you will need to sell your house for a certain number. You decide to call a real estate agent to help determine a likely selling price.

Who do you call? Well, three people come to mind: Sally from your softball team; Bart, who lives next door; and Edgar, who has the full-page local magazine ads and seems to rule the bus bench kingdom. These real estate agents are top of mind because you KNOW them. They are TOP OF MIND.

Like

You imagine reaching out to each of them to ask for help and think about whom to call. Sally from the softball team is friendly and supportive on the field. You *like* her. Bart from next door is a good guy too. You remember the time he offered to water the plants while you were out of town. He's always waving and smiling. He's a pretty *likable* guy. Come to think of it, that Edgar guy from the bus benches is cool too. He's always giving money to sponsor charity events, and he even sponsored your softball league.

Trust

You know and like all three of these agents. They all seem like good people. You wouldn't necessarily trust them with your life, but they seem honest enough to help you value and sell your house. Each of them has been in the community for a while now, and you think they would have been run off years ago if they weren't reasonably *trust*worthy.

You have a dilemma. You KNOW, LIKE, and TRUST each of these people. They are each top of mind. Of the 30,962 potential real estate agents in the state, you've narrowed your choice down to three. But now what?

One option is to interview all three and hire the best or the cheapest. In my hardcore networking days, I was commonly asked to compete in these situations. I was one of the three agents called in to interview for a listing because I was top of mind. I met a lot of people at events where I took their business card, entered it into a database, and added them to my mailing list. They heard from me once a month, then once a year or so I might invite them to one of my famous breakfast meetings, where I would reMIND them about my expertise and success. The breakfast meeting was always about one thing for me: How do I make sure I make an impression and stay top of mind with this person?

This strategy worked well enough. My business grew to a certain point, but the real estate agent persona was exhausting. Winning smiles and firm handshakes were draining. "Modeling" myself after more successful agents was really just fancy talk for pretending to be someone I wasn't. Faking it to belong had almost killed me. I simply couldn't afford to make the same mistake again.

I'm glad I found a better way.

The Top of Heart model

Head (mindset)

As you continue mulling over the three agents to help with your out-of-state move, you remember the time you lingered with Sally in the parking lot after practice one Thursday night. You just happened to park next to each other, and as you were about to collapse into your cars after an extra hard batting session, Sally looked over the top of her car at you and asked how your mom was doing. She remembered that you missed the last practice because you had flown home to help your mom move to an assisted living facility. "How's your mom doing with her new living arrangement?" Simple but impactful. With her genuine inquiry, Sally was demonstrating an interest in you on a human level. She was *connecting* with you, *human to human*, beyond the context of your relationship (softball). It wasn't just about her experience or your experience, standing there in that lot, it was about OUR experience (me to we). Her mindset was relational rather than transactional.

As humans, we are biologically driven to form social connections. In his book *Social: Why Our Brains are Wired to Connect*,[8] Matthew D. Lieberman writes that "people's need to connect with others is even more basic than food and shelter and is the primary motivation of one's behavior." In fact, Lieberman reveals: "The importance of social connection is so strong that when we are rejected or experience other social 'pain,' our brains 'hurt' in the same way they do when we feel physical pain."

Meanwhile, and with a similar mindset, Bart had also *connected* with you. One Sunday morning, he knocked on your door with a look of concern on his face. "Hey, neighbor. I notice your yippy fluffball hasn't been alerting me to the FedEx truck. Is he okay?"

That little fluffball had gone to doggy heaven (of natural causes), and all was quiet and a little lonelier in the house. Downright depressing, in fact. Bart was truly concerned when he heard the news, knowing that you had a very close bond. He surprised you with a chocolate cake and a sweet card the very next day. He recognized the pain of a fellow human being, and he even remembered that this particular human happens to love chocolate cake. His mindset was all about *connecting* with you, *human to human*, beyond the context of your relationship (neighbors). Suddenly you weren't two neighbors looking over your fence at each other (me); you were two humans sharing a moment of grief (we). Now that's a powerful mindset indeed.

Why is this? Grief is a type of human vulnerability, and true, authentic connection requires vulnerability. World-renowned author and speaker Brené Brown, LCSW, PhD, said in her TedTalk on the subject: "In order for connection to really happen, we have to allow ourselves to be seen, really seen."[9] This is so true! Being seen moves people out of the checkbox of being nothing more than a number, a sales statistic, and tells them: "I see you; I value you; I want to connect with you." And on our side of the relationship, it requires that we show up as a person, with all our vulnerabilities in tow. To quote the remarkable Brené Brown again, "Because true belonging only happens when we present our authentic, imperfect selves to the world, our sense of belonging can never be greater than our level of self-acceptance."[10] As I always say, we cannot enjoy a sense of belonging in the world until we find that belonging with ourselves. I never seemed to fit in because I couldn't accept myself.

Meanwhile, unlike super-connector Bart, Edgar had *connected* with you only once. You were on a local non-profit board together and Edgar had invited you out to lunch. As a new board member, you were excited to get to know a colleague. Unfortunately, Edgar didn't even wait for the ice waters to hit the table before launching into his clearly scripted dialogue, crafted to impress, about all his listings and top-producing real estate accolades. He was happy to tell you all about his sales records, how much he spent on marketing, and where he was going on vacation, but he didn't take the time to ask about YOUR business, YOUR family. In fact, he didn't show any interest in you as a human being. He pretended to ask about you, but he didn't listen to your answers.

He clearly didn't care. His mindset had one focus – himself. He didn't achieve a *genuine human connection.*

In her book *Attachment Theory in Practice*, Susan M. Johnson, EdD, writes: "The key factors that define the quality of an attachment bond are perceived as accessibility, responsiveness, and emotional engagement."[11] You probably weren't feeling much of any of those three things from Edgar.

You hadn't thought about it at the time, but when you remembered the lunch, you realized YOU were the one on the menu – just a piece of sales quota meat. If you're like most people, you don't like being served up to the altar of the sales trophy gods. You won't be calling Edgar to sell your house because Edgar failed to connect with you, *human to human*, beyond the context of your relationship (board member colleagues). It was all about him (me me me), never about you, and there was no shared experience (no we). That's a mindset that creates differences and boundaries (not the healthy kind) and prevents connections.

Hands (skillset)

Sally had shown empathy and vulnerability; she had gotten real and revealed herself as a truly human being. Imperfect and flawed, she wasn't hiding behind job titles, class structures, or societal roles. Sally showed up as Sally in every interaction. And Sally was highly skilled – a true high performer. Sally operated at the highest level with consistency and excellence. She had the required skillset. In fact, she had more than enough proficiency and demonstrated excellence at every turn. Sally had developed a level of mastery in her work that can only come with time, attention, and deliberate practice.

As your relationship deepened over time, Sally raised capital for you – *social capital*. Robert Putnam, Stanfield Professor of International Peace at Harvard University, defines social capital as "connections among individuals – social networks and the norms of reciprocity and trustworthiness that arise from them."[12]

At one point, while you were building your career, Sally took the time to methodically scroll through her contacts and pluck out the names of people who could help you. She was generous with her own social capital, making important introductions and lending her considerable clout to your name. In this way, she became an important ambassador, a significant *investor* in your career. Her own excellence extended to her network; after all, like attracts like, and her referrals reflected this.

Bart continued to connect with you, but never outside your one-on-one boundary. You didn't share friends or acquaintances, or really anything outside of your direct relationship. It was a nice enough human connection, but the long, deep thread that runs through a more profound relationship was missing. When it came time to check out Bart by asking around and looking him up online, you found broken links on his website and no proof that he actually had the skills required to sell your house effectively and for the most money. Indications of excellence were missing entirely. Bart was a great guy with a great mindset, but he failed to demonstrate that he had the goods to get the job done.

Heart (heartset)

As you and Sally invested in each other, the strength of your shared experience grew. Your relationship became a joint venture of sorts, and you teamed up at times to invest in others. You became social capital partners, on the lookout for smart investments that could further your common causes, your shared loves, or your hope for more joy. You were aligned in spirit through your community of values, dreams, beliefs. You were bound by an emotional attachment, true to each other, and true to the new entity that emerged from your joint venture – a relationship that bore its own identity separate from your individual identities. You could say you shared a common "heartset." You belong with Sally and she belongs with you. Not in a romantic sense, of course, but in a "we" sense.

So rather than making the effort to interview a bunch of real estate agents, it was like reaching into your pocket and pulling out the obvious choice when you looked over at her one day and simply said, "Hey, Sally. Mind coming over to discuss my move when you get a spare moment?"

The Top of Heart worldview doesn't require that we do away with marketing funnels, ads, and sales calls. Top of Heart doesn't need us to drop the processes; it just calls us to a higher pitch. It engages us to do more important work. It lifts us to a bigger purpose, with more meaning, then sets us down into what is real and true and human.

As I got real in recovery, my new worldview began to carry over into real estate, and suddenly I had more business than I could handle. I was showing up as the imperfect, flawed Grant. I also brought all my passion and enthusiasm with me. Instead of dimming my light to fit into the real estate agent persona, I let my truth shine. The guy you met in the 12-step meeting was the same guy you met when you needed to sell your house. You might say I was finally mastering the dance between happiness and living in congruence with one's values.

PART FOUR: HEAD, HANDS, AND HEART

CHAPTER 16.
HEAD (MINDSET)

Cut the bullshit. Really.

Does the following sound familiar to you?

There you are, innocently minding your own business on LinkedIn, engaging with other people's posts and adding witty comments, and it happens – a connection request immediately followed by a sales pitch. It goes a little something like this:

"Grant, I want to be respectful of your time."

Ugh... DO you??? Alarm bells are already going off in my head, but I continue reading anyway, giving them the benefit of the doubt.

"I came across your profile and wanted to reach out. I've recently helped many key decision-makers enhance their business's safety, security, and remote site monitoring. Technoblahblah's integrated security camera, alarm, environmental sensor, and access control solution is helping executive leadership and businesses stay proactive and secure. Do you have ten minutes coming up? Feel free to leave your email, and I'll reach out ASAP!"

No, sir, you do not want to be respectful of my time. No, sir, you may not have my email address. No, sir, I do not have ten minutes coming up.

In this scenario, I am the prospect, the prey, the mouse to be trapped. I am clearly one of many in a numbers game I didn't ask to play. This eager hunter is pursuing me for the same reason hunters have hunted since the beginning of time – to take meat back to the family. I don't want to be the family dinner, and I'm guessing you don't either.

As annoying as it is to get cold called, shoved into sales cycles, and tricked into endless manipulative selling loops, I get it. As marketers and salespeople, we inherit these tips from our sales trainers and managers, who inherited them from their sales trainers and managers, and on and on the cycle continues.

I've personally been guilty of the same manipu-marketing in days gone by. I would post a house for sale on Facebook with a few photos and scant detail. The "lead" clicks the link to see the price or other pertinent information, then the lead faces a hostage scenario: give up their email address and phone number or see no details. The lead reluctantly pays the ransom (hands over their personal data), realizes the house is not for them (not even close to their desired budget or area of town), and closes the window. Most people have a "junk" email address especially for these purposes. Most people just enter a fake number. And for those that use a real number, they are certainly not receptive when that number is called. No one wins: I didn't get a lead, and the consumer is plain irritated with me. Any reasonable person would be irritated.

We all see the trickery of these sales approaches, and we see through the artificial pleasantries, yet we continue to cling to these desperate attempts at "marketing." Can you imagine if we did this on a dating site? "You can see my photo, but to see more than the main photo and the details of my profile, you have to give me your phone number so I can call and ask you out."

Uh, no thanks. There is a time and a place for each of these strategies when executed with care. Too often, however, there is no care involved. This is where the know–like–trust of top of mind doesn't quite stand on its own two feet.

Know

When we are *known*, our sales will improve. We are taught to "get in front of" as many people as possible so that they *know of us*, so that they are *aware* of us. But awareness of someone and knowing someone are two different things.

I sent out postcards for years so people would "know of me." This created awareness, but it didn't help people *know* me. And on the rare occasion that the postcards got the phone to ring, we were still strangers.

My friend Oscar is a top insurance salesperson in town. His bright red storefront cannot be ignored. He's been complaining to me lately that his sales aren't improving, in spite of being well *known* in town.

The truth is that Oscar is not well *known*. People are aware of him because they all drive by his bright red office with his name plastered all over it, but they do not *know* him. Oscar prefers crunching numbers over building relationships. Since they don't *know* him, they certainly can't *like* him.

Awareness is a great start, but it's not enough.

Like

When people know of us but don't *know* us, they might have a favorable opinion of us, but they can't really *like* us.

Trust

When we are in front of a lot of people rather than with people, there is no opportunity for real trust to form.

It's certainly okay that Oscar prefers numbers, but he may need some help with sales and marketing if he plans to grow his business with a top-of-mind approach. If he really wants to grow like crazy, he might benefit from adopting an entirely new way to look at the world.

Top of Heart worldview

A Top of Heart worldview begins with our mindset (our head), because a Top of Heart approach is not about what we are doing but who we are being. It's the mindset of connecting in an authentic manner, person to person. To connect in this way, we must get clear about who we are, then we can bring who we are into each interaction. We are with people rather than in front of people. Top of Heart is about finding what is most true and beautiful in ourselves and sharing it with others. This is the way we have actual relationships that serve us all.

And the "secret" is *actual relationships*. People, not leads.

Many studies show that addiction is about lacking that human connection. It starts early in life. In his book *In the Realm of Hungry Ghosts: Close Encounters with Addiction*, Dr. Gabor Maté cites multiple studies showing that children who experience disruptions in human connection (attachment, neurobiologically speaking) develop a different biochemical climate in their brains from children who do not experience those attachment breaks.[13] This altered mental climate affects how they interact with their environment, creating less flexibility and adaptability and hampering their overall health and maturity. As a result, they become more vulnerable to addiction.

Fittingly, addiction has long been described as the disease of isolation – physical, emotional, psychological isolation. I get this.

As I sat in those 12-step meetings hiding my true self, I was a two-timing cheater. I was cheating myself of any hope for growth, and I was cheating my fellow recovering addicts from really seeing me. I was withholding myself from the community by refusing to give what is most valuable – my true self. I learned that my recovery, my freedom, my survival would require me to get more real than I had ever been – with myself and with my community.

As I journaled like crazy, working through the 12 steps, I came to understand my desperate search for belonging. When we came to the US from South Africa, I was a scared little boy who was rejected by classmates and labeled an outsider – the worst possible mark on any kid on a playground. That rejection was traumatic. I spent the rest of my life protecting myself from a second serving of that trauma. I fought to avoid rejection at all costs, and it wasn't easy. After all, I was gay, and just a little weird and awkward too.

I tangled and twisted myself to avoid rejection. I did whatever was necessary to fit myself into the right shape. And when I knew that fitting in would be impossible, I made sure I stood out to such a degree that no one would even consider inviting me to the fitting-in party. In other words, I rejected the group before they could reject me.

Can you think of a time you preemptively rejected someone or something to protect yourself?

But then it was time to get clean or die. In those 12-step meetings, I was faced with a life-or-death choice: become a part of the group or die. Get real about who I really am, for the first time in my life, or slither back onto the streets and play out the slow, painful death that's waiting for me. I'm not sure I would have ever found the courage to get real if I hadn't been faced with this ultimatum from hell. But I'm here to tell you: There is no need to wait for such a dramatic choice. Getting real is the only way to happiness and fulfillment. And in sales and business, getting real is the only way to true success and fulfillment.

Are you willing to twist yourself into a pretzel as I did to find your success?

or

Would you rather show up as you *really* are and gain access to the ultimate fulfillment?

When I switched my mindset from "how do I get this person to do what I want (buy something)?" to "how do I bring all of me to this relationship and really show up for this person?" a big shift happened. As I developed true relationships, I found my community – my place to belong.

We build community one relationship at a time. As we build community, we build social capital. When we have disposable social capital, we invest that capital in our communities. This investment adds tremendous value. As we add tremendous value, we receive tremendous value. The social capital compounds. Welcome to the Top of Heart virtuous cycle.

The benefits of social capital act as a two-way street. Community building has been shown to improve our mental state. A 2022 study in *Current Opinion in Psychology* suggested that "building, restoring, and sustaining social identities through meaningful group-based connections" can ward off loneliness and provide overall mental health support.[14]

A 2011 study in the *Journal of Happiness Studies* also supported the notion of "social capital as an important piece in predicting happiness."[15]

This supports the idea that, by compounding social capital, a Top of Heart worldview can also compound mental health capital as well. It begins with getting real. "Start with WHY" has it all wrong. We need to start with WHO. It's not about what we need to do to reach our goals but WHO we need to become and WHO we need to enlist in the vision.

For instance, my insurance salesperson friend Oscar might benefit from enlisting a sales partner in his vision, someone who would love to form new relationships in the community to build on the awareness that Oscar has created.

WHO are you being called to be?

Yes, I have to mention the "A" word: A-U-T-H-E-N-T-I-C-I-T-Y. This powerful call to action has been diluted by corporate speak, social media buzzword, and coachy pop psychology for years. As a result, this important concept has been watered down and dumped into the trash heap of phrases so overused that we've forgotten their true meanings.

But let's get real. REAL. Being authentic means being willing to be seen as we really are, in all the ways that might make us proud or might make us feel vulnerable. Real life is not social media; we don't get to choose only the highlight-reel stuff. Being real means modeling after those we admire without copy-pasting their personalities. Being real means loving our differences, even the less attractive, more awkward ones. It's okay that your voice has that funny squeak when you get excited. It's okay that you snort when you laugh. We all have our thing. For instance, I get so engrossed in conversation when touring houses with clients that I've been known to walk into my fair share of walls. It's okay. In fact, it's more than okay. These silly things are endearing. These personal peccadillos actually create greater trust.

Recently, a friend of mine was searching for a family therapist to help with some issues they were working through at home. They met with three therapists and chose one rather easily. I asked why they made the choice they did and they said, "Well, this is going to sound crazy, but we chose Linda because she spilled coffee on herself in the first five minutes of our meeting. The way she laughed at herself and then moved right on was so humble, and somehow we knew this was someone we would feel more comfortable sharing our private lives with. The other two therapists were intimidating; they were just a little too perfect."

What are the silly/embarrassing things about you that you can embrace and laugh about? Afraid of revealing such vulnerability, especially in a business situation? Do you worry it would make you appear less credible? Harvard Professor of Organizational Behavior Jeff Polzer disagrees with this assessment. In a 2018 interview with business writer Daniel Coyle, Polzer explains:

"People tend to think of vulnerability in a touchy-feely way, but that's not what's happening. It's about sending a really clear signal that you have weaknesses, that you could use help. And if that behavior becomes a model for others, then you can set the insecurities aside and get to work, start to trust each other and help each other. If you never have that vulnerable moment, on the other hand, then people will try to cover up their weaknesses, and every little microtask becomes a place where insecurities manifest themselves."[16]

Some people in business might not be aware of this. They put on their sales hat and suddenly their humanity slips away. They put on their sales hat and suddenly their empathy slips away. They put on their sales hat and, bit by bit, they adopt a completely different personality.

"Real estate agent Grant" was necessary when I first started in real estate. I was also "recovering addict Grant," "living in a storage unit Grant," and "still on probation Grant." Bringing "all of myself" to my work was not an option. But as I worked through the 12 steps and came clean with myself, I discovered that there was so much more to me than those labels. As I learned to tolerate myself, and eventually to like myself little by little, I was able to shed the real estate agent persona. I could just be Grant, perhaps for the first time in my life.

We are here on Earth to connect deeply, honestly, and for the long term with people who we actually care about. The length and width of our relationships don't need to be defined by the sales transaction. It's exhausting donning a persona to work every day. That's what makes it feel like work – maneuvering through your career under the weight of that carefully crafted identity.

Sophia recently shared with me at lunch that she's quitting her job as a high school principal. She loves education, she loves the kids, and she loves the work. So why is she resigning? "I'm simply exhausted from playing this ridiculous 'principal' role all day every day. From the moment I get to work until the time I leave, I have to be ON. I'm worried that I'll be disrespected or outright rejected if I'm *all of me* at work. So instead, I just 'play principal' all day and I'm so bored!"

The Top of Heart mindset creates a world where smiles come more easily, life becomes more balanced, and long, leisurely conversations about everything but business are incredibly profitable. This is a world where joy and profit are tightly tethered.

In this new world, they are not mutually exclusive. In fact, they yearn for each other. Joy doesn't live in the old point-and-shoot sales maneuvers; it's not fun to sell that way, and it's certainly not fun to be sold to in that way.

When I was a lonely third grader in a new world I didn't belong to, I started roller skating for fun. I spent hours after school skating alone in a nearby church parking lot. The smooth blacktop seemed as if it had been created for the ultimate glide. I taught myself to skate backward and even to do some simple little spins. I pretended I was dancing on ice, as I had seen the glamorous glitter people do on TV.

One day, I noticed a neighbor watching me through her blinds. I was super embarrassed and immediately changed up my routine – less spins, less "dancy" moves, more boyish speed skating. I didn't enjoy this as much, but I skated this way for the rest of the afternoon. Somehow I knew that my more feminine moves would be frowned upon. As I skated home, right past the house with the nosey neighbor, I glanced over at the window only to realize that the "lady" was actually a plant on a stand. I had changed my entire skating session to please an imaginary woman.

Embrace what makes you different. Be courageous enough to show up as you really are, claiming your worthiness. Showing up this way is perhaps the hardest part. We are so much stronger when we allow our differences to take us to new heights instead of new lows. Do it for YOU. Stop performing for people who aren't even watching you!

Dig deep, get real, and forge your very own unique path in the service of others. This mindset is key to living an inspired and rewarding Top of Heart life.

Reader exercises

"Head" focuses on the mindset shift from transactional to relational. This mindset shift comes when we get real, present, open, and helpful. The following table makes each

**of these aspects accessible to you, the reader, with questions
and action practices.***

**A note about the action practices: Each of these practices have varying levels of
depth and intensity. In some cases, a simple journaling session will suffice. In others,
you may want to consider coaching, therapy, and other guided experiences to achieve
the best results. Above all, remember that this is a lifelong journey. They are called
"practices" for a reason; be patient with yourself.*

Getting real		
Aspect	**Questions**	**Action practices**
It's not about *what* we are doing but *who* we are being.	What makes you happiest? What brings you joy? What brings you pride?	See the list of core values at www.topofheart.com/values >Note the ones you feel apply to you (feel, don't think). >Now highlight the 5–7 values that inspire you the most. >Write these values (with a descriptive sentence if you like) and place them where you will see them each day. *Example: I set a calendar reminder with my values so that I see them each morning.*
It's not about what we need to do to reach our goals but WHO we need to become and WHO we need to enlist in the vision.	When does your heart feel fullest? How would you like your friends and family to describe you? What character traits will be required to achieve what you want?	See the list of strengths at www.topofheart.com/strengths >Think about times you have felt particularly confident, capable, and successful. >Which of these strengths were you utilizing?

		>Choose 5–7 of your favorites. >Keep this list of strengths with your list of values. You will deploy these strengths to help you live your values.
It's about getting real about who we are and getting clear about our beliefs.	What are five adjectives your friends would use to describe you? What inspires you about the world we live in/the people of the world? When do you feel most alive? What beliefs are present when you feel this way? *Example: I feel most alive when I'm parachuting out of airplanes – I believe I am brave and I have control over my own destiny.*	>Establish a regular stillness practice – this could be yoga, meditation, or simply a designated time to be still. >Create a space for yourself that silences as much external noise as possible. This can be a solitary walk, a park or other place in nature, or a dedicated corner of your home. >Get quiet and still. >Make note of beliefs that arise. Your thoughts often contain your underlying beliefs. >Identify the beliefs that support your values or strengths. >Add these beliefs to your list of strengths and values.

| It's about loving our differences. | Who are your heroes and what are the characteristics you admire in them?

What makes them unique?

What makes you unique? | >First, think about the ways you tend to approach tasks and interact with others and take note of what sets you apart.

Example: You tend to be super methodical.

>Next, ask for feedback from friends, family, and colleagues. Ask for their observations about what makes you unique.

>Make a list of the differences you notice that are also noticed by others.

>Circle the differences you are most proud of.

>Add these to your list of strengths, values, and beliefs. |

Getting present		
Aspect	**Questions**	**Action practices**
Practice mindfulness.	Are you fully attentive and aware in this moment? Have you let go of distractions? Have you taken ownership of the energy you are bringing into this moment?	>Sit quietly, even for just 30 seconds. >Look around you and notice the colors, textures, and sounds. >Now close your eyes. What is distracting you from this moment that you can release?

		>Focus on the thing you want to release (whether an event, a thought, a relationship, or a self-limiting belief). Visualize letting it go, perhaps putting it into a balloon and setting it free into the sky, never to be seen again.
		>Now that this distraction is released, name the energy that you want to create in this new moment, e.g., excitement, love, joy, peace.
Connect human to human and shift your thinking from transactional to relational.	How can you be more present in conversations? Are you focused on the relationship or the potential sale? Are you allowing your true personality to show through or hiding behind your job role?	>Remove your phone from the table at a restaurant. >Preview the menu online so you can focus on relationship building instead of what you're going to order. >Make sure you finish your food first (this means you were talking the least). >Make it a habit to ask follow-up questions throughout the conversation. *Example: "You moved here to be closer to family? How does it feel to have your mom and dad just down the street? Are the kids enjoying having their grandparents so close too?"*

| Become aware of opportunities. | Are you fully focused on the conversation? Are you listening with a curious and open mindset? Are you paying attention to the meaning and context of what is being said? | >Pay attention to non-verbal cues such as facial expressions and body language, tone of voice, or changes in volume or speed. >Practice suspending your own judgment and listening without jumping to conclusions. >Show true interest with your facial expressions and other body language. >Ask clarifying questions to get to the heart of the matter. |

Getting open		
Aspect	**Questions**	**Action practices**
Demonstrate personal courage.	Are you allowing your personality to shine through? Are you speaking up for yourself when it's important? Are you willing to be candid, even when it may not be popular or easy?	>Review your list of strengths, values, differences, and beliefs. Choose one or two to practice at a time. *Example: Have a quirky sense of humor? Practice sharing that sense of humor in your interactions.* >Take an emotion inventory. Set an alarm that goes off a few times a day and then journal which emotions you're experiencing when the alarm goes off. This will help you get in touch with your feelings.

		>Share your feelings with one other person each day to become comfortable with speaking up for yourself and how you are feeling. >Practice being candid by listening during conversations with people who have a different perspective. Practice saying, "I hear you. I have a different perspective. May I share my point of view with you?"
Show love and kindness.	Do you show appreciation? Are you a source of support and care? Are you patient and understanding?	>Think of a relationship you would like to strengthen. Imagine ONE action you can take today to demonstrate appreciation. >Choose a relationship you would like to nurture. Seek an opportunity to lend your support. Sometimes you can pay attention to find the best way to support and sometimes you will need to simply ask, "How can I support you in this?" >Is there a relationship in your life that you find challenging? Write three ways that you can show more patience and

		understanding toward this person and the relationship, then practice being more patient. *Example: I will stop interrupting my son when he goes on a rant. I will listen fully and see if I can understand his perspective more clearly.*
Be seen as you are.	Are you living consistently with your values and beliefs? Are you expressing your thoughts and feelings openly? Do you understand how others are perceiving you?	>Check your list of values versus your current personal and business goals. Are they aligned? If not, adjust your goals until they reflect your values. *Example: If your goal is to be available 24/7 for your clients and your value is to be present with your family, you may not be aligned.* >Practice using "I" statements in your conversations about your feelings. >Choose a trusted friend and practice sharing your thoughts and feelings. Start small with less risky conversations and gradually work your way up to more vulnerable topics.

		>Ask your trusted friend how they perceive you. Remain open and non-defensive. Write down key words they say. Check those key words against your values list and decide if you want to make any adjustments.
Build community.	Diverse communities are strong communities. What are ways you can make your circle more inclusive? What are the values, beliefs, and strengths you want to build your community around? What is your communication plan?	>Choose three people in your circle who are from a different culture or background than you. Spend time with them one on one. Get to know them. If appropriate, ask them directly how you can be their ally. >Identify key members of your circle. Invite them to develop the group's key values with you. Brainstorm together. >Create a simple process for communicating with the group (how often and what format) and responding to feedback.

Getting helpful		
Aspect	**Questions**	**Action practices**
Approach each relationship with a fresh perspective.	How can you help them overcome personal or professional obstacles? How can you help them get what they want? How can you be helpful in the challenging moments?	>Choose one person who is facing a challenge. Ask how you can help them. If they would like some assistance, help them develop a simple action plan (identify the next best two to three action steps). >Share your connections. *Example: Do you know someone who is an expert that could help?* >Share your expertise. Do you have skills or knowledge that can help them achieve their goal?
Build and invest your social capital.	How can you create opportunities for others? Where can you volunteer and share your social resources? Where can you strengthen your relationships to build further social capital?	>Choose your three favorite vendors or small business connections. Ask them what a good referral would be for them. Set an outgoing referral goal – how many referrals would you like to send them this month? Write the goal with your other business goals. >Choose a favorite cause. Reach out to a non-profit that supports this cause and ask them about what resources or connections they would find helpful. Consider your relationships and

		make connections that will help.
		Example: The non-profit needs to update their website, and you have a relationship with a website developer who is willing to do some work for free or low cost for a good cause.
		>Identify five additional types of people you would like to add to your circle.
		Example: You might need a certified public accountant or divorce lawyer in your network, or you might be seeking someone that can add some fun or is an outdoor enthusiast.

CHAPTER 17.
HANDS (SKILLSET)

I wasn't suffering from impostor syndrome; I was an impostor.
Early in my recovery journey, as I finally learned to get real
and honest, I had to face a painful truth: I was beginning to learn
who I was and where I wanted to go, and I realized that I didn't
have the skills to get there. I had copied the professional personas
of every guru, author, and sales manager I wanted to emulate. I
was hiding behind a hastily prepared personality that was shaped
from my imagination to resemble "Grant the real estate agent." I
was a real estate agent impostor.

I wasn't trying to con anyone. I was living a clean, honest life.
I had stopped scheming and scamming for drugs. I was working
hard to build my real estate practice, and I had a genuine interest
in serving my clients at the highest level.

According to Candice Kingston, author of *Your Impostor
Moment: Breaking Through the Barriers of Self-Doubt*: "Impostor
moments crop up when we doubt our abilities. What happens
if you don't know what you're doing? If you really cannot do
the thing you were talking about or don't have experience, does
that make you a true impostor? The fact is, no one is perfect, or

knows every little thing about the subject. That doesn't make us all impostors; it makes us all human."[17]

But my "training" in the industry was the standard training at the time. I was taught to "fake it till you make it."

The phrase "self-fulfilling prophecy," a seemingly close cousin of "fake it till you make it," came about in 1947 when Robert Merton, considered a founding father of sociology, defined it as "a false definition of the situation evoking a new behavior which makes the originally false conception come true."[18]

How much happiness and fulfillment can we realistically expect to derive from a situation that, by definition, originates as fake, creates a new behavior that is fake, and creates a new outcome that is – you guessed it – fake? This might be a popular, catchy sounding approach in business, but how much confidence can it instill? A house built on a shaky foundation is not a house that I would ever want to sell.

"Fake it till you make it" also does not inspire confidence in others. A study documented in the *Journal of Management* found that "exaggerated self-enhancement" in a work environment had "negative indirect effects" on trust among coworkers.[19] The study described the impact of this variation of "faking it" as "universally negative" and stated that it lowers job performance, presumably from the atmosphere of distrust created. Imagine how your clients feel as you're "faking it."

So we have now established that creating relationships based on a shaky foundation of distrust creates a self-fulfilling prophecy of distrust that is proven to negatively impact work performance. But how does "fake it till you make it" affect you on a personal level?

Noted clinical psychologist Carl Rogers made significant discoveries regarding the incongruity ("inharmoniousness") of our various selves. In *Personality Theories*, Dr. C. George Boeree writes: "This gap between the real self and the ideal self, the 'I am' and the 'I should' is called incongruity. The greater the gap, the more incongruity. The more incongruity, the more suffering.

In fact, incongruity is essentially what Rogers means by neurosis: Being out of synch with your own self."[20]

Neurosis from the incongruity of behaving in a way that does not align with your authentic self? Been there, done that, and it almost killed me. No thank you!

When we want to "close leads," "fake it till you make it" works well. When we want to "serve people," as we do with the Top of Heart worldview, "fake it till you make it" is not good enough.

Sitting in a wildly popular real estate class, I was taught to write daily affirmations in the present tense: "I earn $200,000 a year and I love it." I filled a page each day. But I knew that the truth was "I live in a storage unit, I'm two months behind on my rent, they are about to padlock the door, and I would be happy to make $20 a day for a few days in a row."

I know affirmations are popular, but let's keep getting real – affirmations without action and skill are just lies we tell ourselves. They are wishes and hopes with no foundation. Writing "I earn $200,000 a year and I love it" 30 times a day won't make it true. I was simply lying to myself. I knew it was a lie on every level.

When someone lies to you 30 times a day, what do you do? You start tuning them out. You ignore them. That's what happens with affirmations without action and skill. This well-meaning but harmful advice about affirmations and "fake it till you make it" mantras has led to the impostor syndrome we hear so much about. If we're fake, we're going to feel fake. It's not a syndrome; it's the truth. When we are faking it, we are impostors.

The power of intention, on the other hand, is proven. Painting a clear picture of where we are heading will aim us in the right direction. Dreams will propel us toward the life that is waiting for us. When we are true to who we are in the moment, our desired outcome comes into focus. When we build on that truth, we create a vision for who we must become to reach that outcome. Intention and dreams are the wings that help us soar.

Dale Schunk, an educational psychologist, has found that our vision of our possible future self is a powerful factor in our achievements. When we believe that we can achieve a particular goal, it has a positive effect on our progress toward that goal. This is why intention is so important. However, Schunk's studies[21] also demonstrate that all the right actions and intentions will not produce the desired outcome without the required skill.

This is why skillset is a key component of the Top of Heart worldview. Without the right skills, we won't get off the ground. We need three core skillsets to create a platform from which we can launch our dreams: strength, personal impact, and excellence.

Strength

Living in that storage unit, newly clean from drugs but now high on Cheetos, Coca-Cola, Marlboro Lights, and four hours of sleep a night, I didn't exactly show up with power and passion during the day. My body had been ravaged from years of endless binges and being routinely up for too many days in a row (if I told you how many, you wouldn't believe me).

I had endless drive and motivation to make a better life, but my body wasn't a willing accomplice. I had burned my healthy hormones to the ground. I had destroyed my receptors, mis-fired all synapses, and drained myself of all serotonin and dopamine. I was still about 30 pounds underweight. My energy matched that of the folks from the nursing home across the street. They were placed in the sun each day as if to recharge, but more commonly to wither, shrivel, shrink. I was coming out of my own Stage 4 withering, but it was a slow process.

My dreams were clear, my vision was intensely focused, but my batteries were dangerously low. Still just in my thirties, I was a dim bulb. Each day, as I pushed toward my future life, I ran out of energy long before I ran out of time. I was faced with the truth that I've heard echoed from loved ones who have suffered grave illness: It's almost impossible to be our best when we don't feel our best.

My experience then was a lesson about energy. It turns out that, when we are healthy, we can choose our energy level. Rather than accepting our energy as it is, we can create our energy. The cigarettes, soda, poor sleep hygiene – it all needed an overhaul. I began to undertake a strength training regime that included body, mind, and spirit.

The roller coaster emotions of early recovery coupled with the roller coaster emotions of an early-stage real estate career were gut wrenching at times. Emotional strength, strength of character, and strength in resilience were all tested often. And as I tested these "muscles," they slowly grew.

Years later, I learned more advanced tools for strength building across all aspects of my life. Strength of body or character isn't enough. We need strength in every area to power our dreams. Strength is a skillset that must be studied, nurtured, and developed.

Without strength, it's hard to find the courage to go deep to figure out who we really are.

Without strength, it's hard to show up as we really are.

Without strength, we fail to act boldly enough to complete our life missions.

What strengths do you need to build to meet your life missions?

"Grant, the truth is that I have enough time. The problem is I run out of energy before I run out of time. I just don't have the strength to follow through sometimes." This recent text from one of my coaching clients says it better than I ever could.

Personal impact

There's a simple formula for personal impact: Helpful + Productive = Personal Impact.

As I emerged from that storage unit eager to build my new life and career in real estate, I had to face an ugly truth that all the affirmations in the world couldn't cure: I was a beginner in real estate and I had terrible work habits. In other words, I was not helpful OR productive. I had passed the real estate exam, but I didn't know the market, the inventory, or the basics of how deals are done. My brain was so tweaked that I couldn't concentrate on the same thing for more than five minutes.

I fought hard to concentrate and learn. If I couldn't get high with drugs, I needed something to help me hide from the shame of my past actions and feel better about myself. I needed to achieve. I needed to win big. But no matter how hard I worked and how hard I chased more sales, success seemed to run faster than I could.

And then it happened: I finished my fourth step. To paraphrase, I made a "searching and fearless moral inventory" of myself. I realized just how broken I was. But I also realized just how common I was. "Just another run of the mill addict," as my sponsor lovingly assured me. I wasn't extra bad or extra special. I realized how human I was.

In the stillness of that truth, I found myself. I found a spiritual connection. And for the first time ever, I found genuine fulfillment. And then it all broke free for me. At work, I found focus as I developed expertise, and I found a deep desire to serve my clients. I was having greater personal impact because the formula was in play: I was productive and helpful.

I learned that personal impact comes from producing fulfillment first and then allowing the right action to follow that fulfillment. It comes about with consistency over extended periods of time. I had spent a lifetime chasing achievement because I thought achievement would bring belonging, love, and fulfillment. It turns out I had it all wrong. Achievement comes from fulfillment.

Once I found satisfaction with what is, more was revealed. As I tuned into my happiness and love, as I amplified my joy, my personal impact multiplied. Looking back, I can see it all clearly.

I was learning to focus on output not outcome. Now, my efforts came from a place of passion rather than a hungry need to fill emotional holes. When we embrace our work and our lives from this place, everything we've ever wanted opens up for us. We grow our impact as we grow from within. Our bold action, derived from fulfillment, becomes the force that propels us forward toward our vision. As we practice action, we tune our skills to the highest possible frequency.

One of the best examples of the value of output over outcome is a highly acclaimed hand-blown glass artist I've gotten to know over the years. When I asked him how on earth he has become so accomplished, he said:

> "Well, I guess I just kept blowing glass year after year, making as much glass as possible that was good enough to sell. I didn't really care about art, I just wanted to sell a bunch of ash trays and plates to pay my bills. Over the years, I played around with new forms, and bit by bit, after screwing it all up enough times, some looks emerged that were sort of interesting. I sold a few so I made a few more. I noticed that I really loved making these pieces. It was just really, really fun. I would totally lose myself in the studio. Many thousands of pieces later, I've developed a style that people are suddenly calling 'art' and paying way too much money for."

With our fulfilled hearts, we operate at a higher frequency. We become experts driven by service rather than greed, and we become much more helpful. Our personal impact grows.

Excellence

I didn't have the luxury of affirmation fairy tales; I had to get real or die. I had to look at the darkest pieces of my personality. I had to face my horrible behavior. I had to drill to the core of my ugliest parts and stare intently into my own soul. And then I had to accept the worst of it. When I made peace with my own depravity, when I surrendered my weapons and gave up the fight, I found the serenity I had been praying for on a daily basis.

I grew my strength and personal impact from that tenuous footing. I took unsure action, I took fearful action, I took the wrong action, and I kept taking action. I took one step forward and two steps back, and sometimes no steps forward and six steps back. And then I fell backward into depths of failure only to be crushed by the rocks that fell in after me.

And then I took action. I remained in motion. Then more action. Nothing motivates like action.

As a brand-new real estate agent, fresh in addiction recovery, it was tough to find clients to show houses to. No one wanted to work with me. I showed myself hundreds of houses instead, practicing endlessly.

Just as fulfillment creates achievement, action creates excellence. Excellence is all about being ready for action and then taking that action. I saw more houses in a week than most agents see in years. I had developed a level of excellence around showings, and this created an excellent understanding of the market and the inventory.

When I finally stumbled into my first clients, I showed up with excellence. In a town of denim and polos, I donned cufflinks and dress shoes (grateful for the thrift store). It wasn't about image; it was about signaling excellence: *I have higher standards and you can expect more from me.*

Excellence is always, every single time – not just when it's convenient.

And still, even with strength and personal impact and excellence, my poor real estate business couldn't quite get the lift it needed to launch into the atmosphere. I would have some decent success, only to fall back to months in a row of no sales. The cufflinks, the enthusiasm, all the personal impact in the world couldn't save me from the sales abyss.

There was still something missing.

Reader exercises

The focus of "hands" is on developing the skillset to bring you from novice to mastery. Hands, aka skillset, consists of building strength, growing personal impact, and creating excellence.

The following table makes each of these aspects accessible to you, the reader, with questions and action practices.*

A note about the action practices: Each of these practices have varying levels of depth and intensity. In some cases, a simple journaling session will suffice. In others, you may want to consider coaching, therapy, and other guided experiences to achieve the best results. Above all, remember that this is a lifelong journey. They are called "practices" for a reason; be patient with yourself.

Building strength		
Aspect	Questions	Action practices
We do better when we feel better. Building strength means building agency over our energy.	If you chose to take the best care of your body, what shifts would you make? Who are the important people in your life that would benefit from your physical self-care? If you had more energy, how would this impact your relationships, your productivity, and your joy?	>Audit your nutritional habits, physical fitness routines, sleep health, mental clarity, and focus. >Next, build supportive habits in each of these areas. >Finally, set goals in each of these areas. >Find experts to help you when you hit an obstacle or plateau.

Greater strength creates greater confidence.	How would your confidence improve if your energy increased? How would your confidence improve if your strength was enhanced? How would your work and life change as a result of a confidence boost?	>Visualization exercise: Close your eyes and imagine walking into a room in the best shape of your life. What would it look and feel like? How would your experience be different from what it is today? >Imagine how you feel. Imagine how you would behave differently as a result of how you feel. Make notes now of any clarity gained from this visualization. >Think of a conversation or interaction you have had in the past 24 hours. Imagine how that conversation would have been different if you had significantly greater confidence. Make note of any positive outcomes you see from this improvement. >Write a description of yourself with the ultimate confidence. Have fun with this. Write as if you are a character in a book. What does the character look like? Be as specific as possible. How do they carry

		themselves? How do they handle challenging situations? Creating a character is a great way to "redesign" yourself from the point of view of an outside, nonjudgmental observer.
Building emotional strength.	What brings you deep love and peace within? Do you have a source for this love and peace? How can you connect to this source on a regular basis?	>Write down the activities that bring you a sense of joy and fulfillment. Circle any that deserve more time on your calendar. Make sure this activity is included in your goals. >Write down relationships that bring you love and peace. Hint: These may be human relationships, but they could also include spiritual connections or even relationships with your fur babies. Circle any that deserve more of your time. >Choose two or three practices that you believe will help you build emotional strength. *Example: Meditation, prayer, journaling, volunteering, art, exercise, therapy.*

		>Choose one to start practicing or to recommit to over the next 90 days.

Growing personal impact		
Aspect	**Questions**	**Action practices**
Personal impact is effective productivity.	What are some ways to focus your production in a way that supports your values and your mission? How can you set your mind on the right targets each day? What habits are supporting you and what distractions are preventing you from practicing these habits regularly?	>Each morning, choose between one and three MUST DO items. These are to-dos that MUST be completed before your head hits the pillow at night. >Write a quick "why" next to each item on the list. >Each night before your head hits the pillow, review your list and assess how you did and what changes you can make to your habits to do even better tomorrow. >See if there are any to-dos you avoided putting on your list today that should go on it tomorrow.

Focus on output over outcome.	How are your habits helping or hurting your progress? Are there any new habits you need to implement? Are there any habits you need to quit?	>Review your current goals. >Under each goal, create three to five actions that you can take toward that goal (they must be actions you can control). *Example: Lose 10 lb. 1. Eat X calories per day. 2. Exercise X days per week. 3. No eating after 7 pm.* >Create a list of good habits that will help you achieve your goal. This is your resource list! Post this list of supportive habits with your goals. >Create a list of habits that are not supporting your progress toward your goals. Circle one and tackle it. >Work on eliminating one unsupportive habit at a time.
Love and joy multiply personal impact.	Who needs you? How would you like to impact them? What energy and emotion would you like to introduce for them today?	>Each morning, choose between one and three people for whom you would like to add love and joy. >Ask: "How can I be a blessing for them today?" Spend some time imagining being in their shoes. Ask yourself what might be valuable for them today.

| | | >Write this item of value next to their name and make it happen. Keep it simple. |
| | | *Example: A quick text saying: "I was thinking of you, how are you? I just want you to know that I appreciate you."* |

Creating excellence		
Aspect	**Questions**	**Action practices**
Excellence is a skill	Are you committed to excellence? How are you growing your excellence skillset each day? How are you practicing excellence?	>Write the top five to ten indicators for excellence in your business. *Example: Our reviews are consistently 4.9 out of 5 or higher.* >Create clearly defined written standards for excellence in all areas of your business. Collaborate with your team so everyone agrees on these standards. >What is one thing you can do in the next 24 hours to increase your excellence? *Example: Hire a coach. Sign up for a class.*

Excellence is a brand.	Have you defined excellence in your life? In your family? In your business?	>Define in writing what excellence means in your personal life, family life, and social life. >Create a common definition of excellence with your team and family. >Choose one area of excellence to build on over the next 30 days. Plan the next three moves to work on. *Example: Marketing. 1. Learn about Instagram. 2. Create a posting schedule. 3. Gather data from this trial and make adjustments.*
Intention + Action = Excellence	What is your plan for excellence? Do you have a plan of action? How will you serve with excellence when opportunity calls?	>Write your intention for excellence in as much detail as possible. Have fun and write out a full vision – what does excellence look like, feel like, etc. >Write down three to five actions you can take in the next 30 days to move toward your written intention. >Review your standards of excellence again (from the previous exercise).

		Imagine different scenarios in your business and how you will be ready to respond with excellence.
		Example: What is your excellence action when you receive a referral from a client?

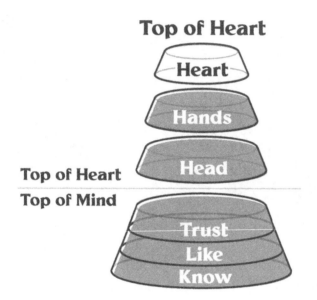

CHAPTER 18.
HEART (HEARTSET)

We are taught from the beginning – from the very moment we enter the world, when we go to school, and when we go to work – that our emotions are not welcome. How many times have you heard a parent utter the "stop crying" command? We are born with explosions of emotion and are steadily drained of these expressions. Chaos would certainly ensue if we all expressed each of our instincts and emotions. There must be some control, but maybe we go too far?

My friend Melinda told me recently, "I noticed myself clamping down on my daughter's anger in an effort to help her meet the mall's expectations of how a little girl should behave. I was trying to help her learn to regulate her emotions. I might have inadvertently taught her that her anger makes her unlovable and she needs to stuff her feelings for my approval... and the world's approval. Yikes!"

Back in my addiction, when I had been awake for three or four days straight with no food, I would enter a place of some freedom from those suppressed emotional states. It was beautiful and free and filled with childlike imagination and wonder. It's sad that I had to get high on meth and sleeplessness to find my emotional truths in the present moment. And believe me, the positive parts of that were quickly overcome by miserable paranoia.

A society cannot progress and maintain wellness for its members if we all sit around in childish emotional states, but we should access these states more often than we do, finding a compromise between robotic and psychotic.

There is a way of being where we can express the best of our emotions with positive outcomes. We can find inner truth, joy, and love and safely share them with others. It is an opportunity to live more fully in the moment, even when we are at work. We can bring the emotional juice to our interactions and experience heightened levels of joy and happiness.

Scientifically speaking, what *does* make people happy? A 2021 study suggests that "autonomy, social support, and generosity lead to greater subjective well-being. Social support and prosocial action such as donations are likely to improve social trust and one's sense of social security, which can lead to greater subjective well-being."[22]

We can increase our happiness, then, by being self-directed, having social support, and being generous (refer back also to the section on social capital). Does this mean that adopting a Top of Heart perspective can increase your own happiness? Read on, continue considering the evidence, and decide for yourself!

Are you ready for that challenge? Are you ready for the call to a Top of Heart worldview, with the emphasis on "heart"?

We can express our excitements and passions rather than holding them down. We don't need to hide our true selves and set our most important feelings aside in the service of our careers.

In fact, Top of Heart insists that your *feelings* are what make you unique. To put this in business speak, your feelings become your differentiators. The excitement and enthusiasm you bring to your projects can be highly marketable. We all want to work with people who are fully engaged and enthused with the projects we've hired them for!

When we become exactly like each other, just one safe, flat monolith, we fail to bring our magnificence to the surface in the service of others. AI has already got sameness covered for us: A + B input = C output. Every time. I've lived so much of my life experience looking in from the outside – first as an outsider from a foreign land, then as a gay "abomination to God," then as an outcast criminal and junky. The unexpected gift of all this is my comfort with being different, unique, the *other*. There is a power and strength in this difference. This vantage point gives unexpected access and perspective.

Do you think Elton John, Lady Gaga, Joan Rivers, and that weird basketball player whose name I can't recall are worried about fitting in? No. They have freed themselves to enjoy and scale their differences to new heights. We can, too.

Differences can be celebrated AND we can create emotional connections, or bridges, to each other. To get clean, I needed to become A PART OF the 12-step community. I needed to join this group to stay alive. But it didn't work until I stopped trying to be LIKE them and stopped trying to impress them so that they'd like me. Communities are more powerful when we are safe to join and connect as we are.

In sales and business we must learn these same lessons, but we seldom do. We are not taught to form the words to express our truth and honor our emotions, our passion, and sometimes even our love for our clients. Instead, we are taught to memorize scripts that have been proven to sell. If all roads in the sales process lead to what the salesperson wants, then it's not selling; it's manipulating. These sales scripts and carefully crafted form letters erect massive barriers between us. They are missing the heart and the humanity. If we found a way to deconstruct these prisons we have created for ourselves, we could find a new way to be, a new way to feel, an entirely new *heartset*.

When we use scripts, it's to accomplish two things: We want to elicit our desired outcome and we want to look good doing it. In other words, we don't want to embarrass ourselves. We want to come across as smart and capable. Scripts lay out a "proven path" for getting what we want. There is nothing inherently wrong with having goals and wanting to look good, and scripts are one way to achieve this. There is a time and a place for scripts, but they do not take the other person's needs into account. When we allow our hearts to lead the way, we lead with empathy and care.

Heartset is an intentional way of being, an approach to business relationships that allows the heart to lead the way. We've done the work with mindset and skillset. We know who we are, we know our capabilities, and now we are ready to show up as we are, in the moment; we are ready to connect. Shedding our professional personas, we step forward as ourselves and allow our own personality to show through. We seek to measure the quality of our relationships rather than the quantity. I learned the hard way during that breakfast fiasco: The sales numbers game doesn't result in many sales numbers! Our prospects and leads don't want to be prospects and leads. They want to be people.

Chatty Connie

Connie was one of my more difficult clients. She was older and didn't use a computer or email. Electronic signatures on documents and contracts were not an option. Connie liked to chat, and each time I went to her house to collect signatures, it always seemed to take longer than the time I had allotted. During the first couple of visits, I did my best to hurry things along. After all, I had a job to do – get the sale of her house to the closing table. This would allow Connie to buy her next house (which we had already identified), and it would allow me to pay my bills – win–win! No matter what I did, my quick stops to get one or two documents signed turned into 45 minutes to an hour. My efforts to move things along more swiftly were futile.

During our third meeting for signatures, something made me pause, look up from my papers, and *see* Connie. She had tears in her eyes. She had been telling her story for a few minutes and her voice had started to break. I began to listen, really listen. Connie was talking about her one true love. He died early in life and, in the 62 years that followed, she never found another to love as she had loved him. She had lived alone, by choice, since her thirties. That's when I decided I should slow down and show up with Connie, in each moment.

Over the coming weeks, I allowed our meetings to run longer and longer. I learned about love and heartache, child rearing, the Dewey Decimal System, and just about everything in between. I learned that Connie made beautiful art and that she volunteered her time at the senior center (she said it made her feel young and beautiful when the older guys flirted with her – OLDER?!!). Connie shared her rich life stories with me, and our times together were transformed from an inconvenient transaction to a transformative life lesson.

My heart grew from our conversations. I realized that there is so much more available in every interaction than what we make room for. Connie died a few years later, and I was grateful for our time together. She taught me to allow for an emotional connection, a new heartset – Top of Heart.

We find Top of Heart moments when we are open to them. Lunch has always been an important part of my business. In fact, I often say, "I lunch for a living." I say this because so many referrals and so much business can be traced back to a conversation started at lunch. I have a specific lunchtime practice that helps guide these conversations toward Top of Heart experiences. It starts with the right heartset.

1. Get intentional

I can't tell you how many times I've been working away at the office only to look up and realize I need to get to a lunch appointment in 15 minutes and it's 20 minutes away. I rush down the stairs (no time for elevators), taking them two at a time, and throw myself into the car. With one motion, the car starts,

184 | Top of Heart

jolts backward, then rockets out of the parking lot and into traffic. Racing to lunch, I take a call to work out an inspection negotiation, for example, only to find out that the deal is about to fall apart because the buyer agent doesn't understand a simple paperwork procedure. REALLY? I share my frustration with the agent, and let's just say it's more like top of lungs than Top of Heart.

As I career into the restaurant lot, I slam on the brakes, end the call with the agent, throw my car in park, and bound out of the car and head first into the restaurant. "I'm so sorry, traffic is awful," I lie (as if my lunch date helicoptered in and that's why they made it on time). Sitting there irritated, sweating up a storm, I'll let you decide what lunch with me might be like that day.

As I've learned the value of Top of Heart connections, I've learned that these connections have the greatest impact when they begin with intention.

In a 2008 publication, Dr Rick Mendius, MD, discusses the origin of the word "intention": "Intention is derived from the Latin root tendere, related to tensum, and therefore to tension and to 'stretching toward,' hence tendencies. It is also clearly related to tend, to tender, and therefore to taking care of and nurturing. These relationships are not linguistic accidents, but point to a deeper species awareness of what intention involves. That which we care about, we foster and repeat."[23]

This is why handwritten cards, invitations to lunch, and birthday celebrations are a core part of my real estate practice; by *tending to* these relationships, I show that I care. Genuinely *caring* is at the *heart* of Top of Heart!

I've now learned to build time into my schedule to let the day breathe. Top of Heart requires adequate oxygen. It needs the space to get real and the safety to show up and allow others to show up as we really are. It needs us to be present with each other so that we can serve at a higher level with our strength, personal impact, and excellence.

I don't make or take calls in the car on the way to lunch now. I listen to music that brings me to a higher state or I drive in silence, focused on my breathing.

When I put my car in park at the restaurant lot, I shut it down and close my eyes. I take at least 60 seconds, and a few minutes if possible, to allow myself to transition. It's a brief meditation where I let what has just happened fade away. I let go of what has been that day, and I visualize the person I'm about to eat with. I set some simple intentions for what I would like to bring to lunch. For instance, "Mary's mom just died. I'm going to be quiet, caring, empathetic," or "Roger just told me on Messenger yesterday that they're having a baby – time to celebrate and bring the enthusiasm!" If I don't know what to expect, that's when I set an intention to remain open and bring my curiosity.

2. Get curious

There are two types of curiosity. One is about how we can serve the person we're with. *I wonder what Josh will need from me today? It will be interesting to see what is going on in his life. I'm curious to know how that new job is coming along. I wonder how he's feeling after the breakup? I wonder how I can add value for Josh today?* Everyone we encounter has a spark that just needs to be lit. Sometimes it's a story, a message, a joke, a hug, or a simple, quiet acknowledgment. With Top of Heart, it's our job to figure out what that spark is. That's where curiosity comes in.

We were discussing curiosity in a coaching session recently, and my client shared the following story:

> "I was in a fender bender last week. Luckily no one was hurt, but it could have been a lot worse. I was pretty shaken up because my entire family was in the car with me. If we had gone through the intersection one millisecond earlier, it would have been a direct hit. When I called my insurance agent to give her a heads up about what happened, she dutifully took down the information

and explained the next steps in the process. I hung up and realized she had never even bothered to ask how we were doing, how we were feeling, nothing. Sure, she knew we were physically unharmed, but it would have been nice for her to be somewhat curious about how this impacted us. I guess curiosity can go a long way."

This curiosity is pretty straightforward; it's just a matter of checking to see how these human beings we care about are doing.

The second type of curiosity is a bit deeper. Now it's time to be still and create a supportive space. The gift we give others is the opportunity to be seen. Really seen. How can I help this person to be seen? We see others as they are, and we honor them just as they are. Therapists call this unconditional positive self-regard, and it holds immense power in relationships. Unconditional positive regard, made popular by Carl Rogers in 1950,[24] initially applied to how therapists should sit with their clients. Now it is being applied to how you can build healthy, strong relationships. The *APA Dictionary of Psychology* defines it as "an attitude of caring, acceptance, and prizing that others express toward an individual irrespective of his or her behavior and without regard to the others' personal standards. Unconditional positive regard is considered conducive to the individual's self-awareness, self-worth, and personality growth; it is, according to Carl Rogers, a universal human need essential to healthy development."[25]

When we create this space for others that is free of judgment and full of appreciation, we begin to forge deeper bonds. We grow and align.

3. Get aligned

I've learned to create the heartset to honor the existence of emotion in the moment. Recently I was lunching with a client. Her house sale was closing in a week and she was packing up to move to Wisconsin. I asked her how the move was going, and

I could feel the heat in her otherwise benign response. "Going well," she said. "It's just a lot."

My response in years past would have been, "Yeah, moving is a bitch." Instead, I said, "A lot? Tell me more."

"You know, family stuff, and we've been in the house a few years. Quite the history."

"History?"

"Well, I'm not sure you know this, but our 18-month-old daughter passed away in that house six years ago. As much as I'm glad to close the chapter on those painful memories, I feel as if in some ways I'm abandoning her in that house."

Heartset is about tuning to the emotional truth in the moment, getting to the *heart* of the matter.

There is emotion – sometimes light and simple, sometimes deep and crushing – threading its way through every interaction, every conversation. Top of Heart is about recognizing that emotional experience and honoring it. When we honor the emotion in the moment and honor the emotion in the relationship, we align our hearts. We go deeper.

Have you ever called the dentist with a toothache? It usually goes something like this: "Hi there, I have a major toothache. It feels as if there's something scraping directly on the nerve. It's excruciating and I would like to come in immediately!"

"Okay, sir. What's your name?"

OKAY?! What exactly is okay about that scenario? Could there be any less acknowledgment of the pain you're in? This is not just a matter of semantics; this is a matter of simple care. Even just "Oh no, may I have your name please?" would have been a start. "Oh no, that sounds dreadful. May I have your name please so we can get you feeling better as soon as possible?" would have been even better.

Sometimes, the emotions are much more subtle, but they still deserve our knowing attention. "Hey, Grant. I got an invoice for $295 from your vendor. We were expecting the $225, but they tacked on $70 for shipping and packaging. Is that right?"

Is that right? Yes, that's part of the program. You have to pay for shipping and packaging. *But did I explain this program fully?* When I'm honest with myself, I realize I didn't explain things well enough. I'm open to the emotion of the moment, and I hear in his "Is that right?" just the faintest hint of irritation. Mistrust. Consumers are all looking for the gotcha, the proof that our trusted advisors aren't really to be trusted.

I see "Is that right?" as a test of our bond. Will I own up to the fact that I didn't explain the program fully? Will I do what is right, without an explicit complaint or request to correct? THESE are golden relationship-building opportunities. We can honor the underlying emotional tone and then answer from that heartset. "No, that is not right. I will cover the $70." No big flare up, no huge deep emotional connection, just a little bridge from "I'm still not sure I can trust you" to "trusted advisor that is now our real estate agent for life."

Think of a time you bought something that immediately broke or otherwise failed to live up to your expectations. How did it feel? Were there moments when you were worried you had been taken advantage of or fooled in some way? That's an awful feeling. As you think about that time, remember how the person who sold you the item or service responded to your concerns. If their response was fantastic, I bet you remember it clearly and it built trust and loyalty. If their response was awful, I bet you still remember it clearly, but it hurt trust and loyalty.

When we are faced with a disappointed or even angry client, it's tough to acknowledge their feelings and respond from the heart. It's much easier to hide behind logic or policies to protect ourselves from our client's heated emotions. Why is that?

The heart is squishy and emotions can be scary to be with. This notion is supported by a 2019 survey conducted by OnePoll with the online therapy business BetterHelp.[26] The survey found that nine in ten people play down their emotions to avoid worrying loved ones. Seven in ten confessed to withholding their feelings from coworkers, friends, and loved ones. And the headline of the survey itself is telling: "1 in 4 Americans feel they have no one to confide in."

Emotions can be scary, so it seems that people avoid dealing with their inherent messiness. Studies further suggest that these feelings of avoidance stem from our beliefs about the nature of emotions – in other words, whether we think of emotions as good things or bad things.

Jill Suttie, Psy.D, writes: "To add to the complexity, we also have beliefs about our emotions—whether they're a positive, manageable force in our lives, or unwanted interlopers that wreak havoc on our psyche. These beliefs may be unconscious, likely based on our own experiences or the implicit and explicit messages we receive from our parents and our culture."[27]

But despite what might be a natural instinct to avoid them, especially the uncomfortable ones, it has been proven that being able to deal with your emotions leads to greater happiness. A 2018 study suggests that accepting rather than judging (and vetoing) our emotions offers broad mental health benefits.[28] And as we've learned, meaningful relationships are key to positive business outcomes.

When we get to the heart of the matter with each other, for better or worse, we get to experience these relationships with each other. Strong relationships improve our well-being. In business, they improve our profits.

Strong relationships start with the heart.

Reader exercises

Heartset is all about "me" to "we." It is getting intentional, curious, and aligned.

The following table makes each of these aspects accessible to you, the reader, with questions and action practices.*

These exercises are built to help you create your heartset as you prepare to spend time face to face with someone,

whether meeting them for coffee, lunch, or a business meeting.

*A note about the action practices: Each of these practices have varying levels of depth and intensity. In some cases, a simple journaling session will suffice. In others, you may want to consider coaching, therapy, and other guided experiences to achieve the best results. Above all, remember that this is a lifelong journey. They are called "practices" for a reason; be patient with yourself.

Get intentional		
Aspect	**Questions**	**Action practices**
Let the heart lead the way.	What are some ways you can set aside the business at hand to care for the person in front of you? How can you be more human in this moment? How can you bring all of you to this moment (feelings AND ideas and thoughts)?	Prepare for a meeting the Top of Heart way: >Check how you are feeling and note your mood. >Decide which pieces of your personal experiences you are willing to share. >Prepare one or two stories that will allow you to safely share your current experience and create a deeper connection.
Create adequate space with empathy.	Who are you about to spend time with? Based on what you know about their life lately, how might they be feeling? What are some of the ways you can show compassion?	>Practice active listening – be present and engaged. >Show compassion with genuine words of support or simple body language. Less is more; trust your instincts. >Be mindful of your own emotions as they come up. Are you feeling judgment or

		discomfort? Acknowledge and renew your focus on them. >Allow for silence in the conversation. >Acknowledge them and let them know they are seen and heard. (Allowing others to be *really* seen is one of the greatest gifts we can give.)
Manage your emotional state and own your energy.	Is there any work you need to do in preparation for clearing your own emotions? How would you like them to feel after your interaction? How should you show up to help them feel that way?	Imagine you are pulling up to a lunch date in your car: >Clear any big emotions. *Example: You may have had an argument on your way to the meeting.* >Practice a clearing meditation. Close your eyes and breathe deeply. Softly repeat "Clear, clear, clear…" as you allow yourself to let go of what has just been. >As you settle down into the moment, visualize how you would like them to feel after your lunch. Set an intention for how you would like to help them. *Example: I want them to feel appreciated.*

		>Plan for how you would like to show up at lunch to help them feel appreciated.
		Example: You may plan to simply look them in the eyes, smile, and say, "Thank you for that help. I truly appreciate you."

Get curious		
Aspect	**Questions**	**Action practices**
Get curious to help in a way that's relevant and useful.	How can you best serve the person you're with? What are their hopes? Dreams? Fears? What do they really need?	>Ask open-ended questions to learn what's in their heart. *Example: "Tell me about what's exciting in your life right now?"* >Practice listening with your heart. Listen to the words AND allow yourself to feel the emotional undertones. Practice listening to feelings, not just thoughts. When you aren't clear about feelings, simply ask. *Example: "How are you feeling about that?"* >Get to the heart of the conversation by asking about their dreams or fears. *Example: "How exciting that Carly is going off to college. What's your dream for her?"*

		>As you feel empathy and compassion in the conversation, pay attention. These moments can be markers indicating an opportunity to connect more deeply.
Curiosity gets us out of our head and into our heart.	Who is this human in front of you? What do they love and hate? What are the values that drive them?	>Shift your focus away from yourself with a simple reminder: "This person in front of me has their own life, dreams, fears, loves. I can't wait to learn more about them." >Choose one or two things you would like to learn about them on a more human level. *Example: What are their passions? Who do they love?* >Listen for any values that drive them. See if you can find out what they stand for.
Curiosity brings us closer.	How can you help this person feel seen and accepted exactly as they are? How can you create space to go deeper with them? How can you allow more emotion into your relationship?	>Look for moments to demonstrate that you hold them in high regard, just as they really are. *Example: "I feel like I just don't have my act together."* *"You are not alone, my friend. Welcome to the human race, haha."*

		>Look and feel for the pause or the moment of light, the glisten in the eye, the break in the voice, the peaceful smile that indicates you have reached an emotional truth.
		>As the emotion comes alive in a conversation, practice moving toward it instead of shying away.
		Example: "That sounds like a scary moment. How have you been feeling since then?"

Get aligned		
Aspect	**Questions**	**Action practices**
Take note of shared significance or emotion in the moment.	As emotion comes up in the conversation, how do you connect with it more deeply to deepen the relationship? Do you have shared goals or a common purpose? Is there opportunity for collaboration?	>Practice acknowledging emotion in a conversation by asking a question. *Example: "How are you feeling about that?"* >Practice acknowledging emotion in a conversation by sharing your observations. *Example: "It sounds like you're feeling frustrated about what happened. Am I right or am I totally off base?"*

		>If you relate to a goal or purpose that is mentioned, say so. Add YOUR emotion. *Example: "I am working toward that end as well, and I'm so excited to know you are too!"* >Once you establish a common goal, suggest a collaboration, if it's appropriate.
Honor the shared emotion and connection in the moment.	How can you honor this shared experience? In what ways are you in alignment? How is your connection deepening?	>Acknowledge any shared experience out loud; this can be deeply meaningful. *Example: "We are both called to serve folks experiencing homelessness," or more simply "Gosh, we both seem to love the same Netflix shows."* >Find a topic and perspective that are significant for you. Share your perspective and how it makes you feel. >Listen actively for alignment on this perspective and these feelings. >Allow emotions (feelings) to exist in the conversation and in the relationship. Acknowledge them without apology.

		Example: "I also feel anxious about the economy. I worry that I'll spend through my savings. This feels scary." Then pause. Leave room for a response. >Practice showing appreciation for your deepening relationship. *Example: "Thank you for letting me share that difficult truth about my situation. It feels encouraging to have you here supporting me as I vocalize my troubles. I appreciate you."*
"Me" to "we."	Is this relationship taking on its own identity? What is the culture of this relationship? What's the next step for this relationship?	Before your next meeting: >Review your list of values, strengths, differences, and beliefs. >Share what you believe are your common values, strengths, differences, and beliefs. >Choose a common perspective that you would like to build on in this upcoming time together. >Set an intention for the next step in the relationship. *Example: This could be a formal collaboration or a double date with your significant others.*

CONCLUSION: SIMPATICO

Sitting in that condo with over $1 million in stock options and all the professional success I could hope for, I was desperately alone. I didn't belong at work. I didn't belong with my friends. I didn't even belong in the condo building. I had subverted my own personality to succeed. I didn't pause to recognize the kid from Africa that needed to be accepted and loved. It was fast forward to achievement at any cost. I thought the achievement would gain me entrance into the belonging club. It would make me acceptable, finally. It would prove my worth.

When we achieve by pretending to be someone we are not, then that success is a fraud. As my dad taught me, when we win by cheating, we are only cheating ourselves. At my core, I was desperately seeking fortune and status to make up for the miserable human being that I was. Perhaps with all that money I would finally belong. *You can stop looking down your nose at me now and judging me behind my back because I earn your annual salary in a couple of weeks.* Well, it turns out it doesn't work that way at all. I just sat in nicer restaurants with friends that were broken like I was. No wonder it all came tumbling down so quickly. Is it any surprise that cocaine had such an immediate grip on me? My brain was a ready vessel for disease; it was already weakened from the trauma of misplacement and terrible self-worth. I have proven that achievement doesn't bring the solution. There are plenty of higher profile versions of my story, and plenty that have ended more tragically. There are far too many rock and sports stars who have died alone and miserable, starving for belonging.

Achievement is beautiful and fulfilling when it is born from our best selves. We can reach new levels of fulfillment when our success is born from who we really are.

Let's turn success on its head. When we find the emotional core of our human connections, we open up to worlds of deeper meaning and higher purpose. When we show up as we really are, our clients are more engaged, enthralled even, and therefore more profitable. They express a sense of ownership in the communities we've created with them. Now we no longer have business and client experiences; we have our experiences.

Great achievement is a beautiful thing on the wings of a fulfilled life. Here we can celebrate our human successes, big and small. I went to see one of my favorite singer-songwriters a few years ago. My husband is not a fan, so I went alone, and I stood in line alone for a few hours to assure a standing-room-only spot right in front of the stage. I went to the show happy with my work, my husband, my life. After a few hours, we lined up at the front of the stage and waited for the show to start. During the wait, I chatted excitedly with the super-fan friends I had met in line. We were high with anticipation, and it was unbelievably exciting to FINALLY connect with fellow freak-level fans for this relatively obscure performer. The show was UNBELIEVABLE and my new friends and I were engulfed in the music together. We all swam together in the pool of that magical evening. We were simpatico.

If I had gone to this show to make me feel better about my life or myself, it might have worked for a short time, but it would have ultimately failed. Of course. Achievement is like that.

The show stood on the shoulders of my love for my life, so it served to multiply my joy. My connections with the super-fans took that joy to an entirely new level. I was prepared to enjoy the show alone, but TOGETHER we reached an entirely new planet. Fulfillment is like that.

In the concert, in my recovery, in my business, I have learned that the source of all that is good comes from one simple shift in my heartset – "me" to "we."

A cross-cultural study on happiness suggests that those of us who attach personal happiness to socially engaging with others experience better subjective well-being.[29] "We" as a prescription for better physical and mental health? I'll take it!

When we move from me to we, the world opens up with new opportunities, unseen wonders suddenly surface, and new talents and powers become available to us. Suddenly we are so much less self-conscious because it's not about us. Suddenly, the most terrified public speakers stand on stage, unafraid, to belt out powerful truths. There is no longer a need to gain approval; approval is something we have given ourselves.

This is fulfillment first. Self-love first. This, ultimately, is how we find belonging. I belong, we belong – when we say we do.

Imagine a world where clients are treated like people. Imagine a world where prospective clients are treated like people and honored simply for their intrinsic value. Imagine these people honored for their emotions and their human foibles along with their magic. Imagine a world with no leads or prospects or sales targets, just people with potential relationships.

Imagine a world where we treated ourselves like people instead of machines of production. Imagine a world where we connect with who we are and how we feel. Perhaps we find a place to forgive ourselves, see ourselves, accept ourselves. When we find that sense of belonging with ourselves, we find a belonging in the larger world, too.

Imagine a world where our highest purpose is a life of fulfillment, an inspired life. Imagine a world where achievement is the sweet surprise, the afterthought that comes from a generous, caring, enlightened life. This is, after all, how the whole thing works: Our greatest achievement pours from our greatest fulfillment.

EPILOGUE: GOING VIRAL

Since this book was born from the disaster I made of my life, it seems fitting that it was also born during a global pandemic disaster. We are starved for community, collaboration, and connection like never before. The Top of Heart movement is coming to town at just the right time.

The Covid-19 lockdowns have wreaked extra helpings of havoc on those with addiction and mental health issues. Isolation is the single most dangerous situation for addicts. As we say in recovery, "An addict alone is in a dangerous neighborhood." That's because when we isolate, we lose a crucial lifeline: a third-party sounding board for our thoughts and a mirror for our actions. We start to believe our own bullshit. At one point during the pandemic, I picked up $1,800 in cash from the bank to buy a used mountain bike. Stacks of cash can be a trigger for me. "Hmm, I wonder if $1,800 would buy an ounce of meth these days," I thought to myself, feeling the weight of the $100 bills and the quickening beat of my heart.

Now that I have a house and a car and some disposable income, I could probably find someone to go pick up drugs for me, and I would only have to deal with that one person instead of a cast of unsavory characters. I could enjoy the highs without the lows. I could finally use meth in comfort (maybe rent a luxury hotel suite to keep things contained and safe), use responsibly, have a phenomenal time, then go back to my regularly scheduled programming. Even as I write this, I can feel my stomach churn slightly with anticipation. I've learned to audit the stuff that comes across my mind. It's what we work on in recovery, and it's part of what we worked on in the mindset chapter.

When I have these thoughts, I look at the thought as if it's a separate entity. I examine it, and then I typically laugh at it, or stomp on it, and snuff it out. But I also speak this bullshit out loud in front of fellow recovering addicts who get me. I call out my thoughts, they nod in silent knowing, and I am seen and accepted. This is the opposite of isolation, and this is how WE save our lives over and over again.

We've learned in our recovery community, and in others, how to gather via Zoom, etc., and we are getting better at it. But that subtle movement in the corner of a mouth, glisten in an eye, or shift in a seat doesn't translate online. These deeply human non-verbal messages are lost. And we are lost. Covid-19 has confirmed what we have always known: People need people in person. We need Top of Heart (head–hands–heart) connections.

It feels poetic that I'm finishing this book about some of my lowest lows in a penthouse suite in Vegas. I needed to get away from the day to day to complete it. A lot of writers choose a quiet cabin in the woods, but I'm not the quiet-cabin-in-the-woods type. It's nighttime, and I'm looking out over the Strip, thinking about past misadventures in this town. I remember a night in the seediest of downtown Vegas hotels trying to blow-dry cocaine that had somehow gotten sweaty during a raucous night at the club. It was as impossible as it sounds, although we certainly gave it our best shot.

There was another night when we were driving through Vegas on the way back to Denver from LA. We had $80 left. It was enough for gas to get home, but certainly not enough for liquor or drugs. And that meant it wasn't enough. So we did what any reasonable addict would do: We gambled it in the hope that we could multiply it into powder. We lost. Do you ever wonder how the people with the "Stranded – need bus tickets home" sign on the side of the road might end up in that predicament? Well, I'm not sure how they got there, but that's how we did.

In the end, I found my way home to myself, a sweeter self from much earlier on.

I almost didn't make it home at all. I never did pay back the drug debt from the beginning of the book. I suppose I've been on the run ever since, putting as much distance between myself and that world as possible.

Here I am today, having more of a cashmere-and-club-soda experience. I have everything I want in life – and more.

How the hell did that hell turn out like this?

I'm 51 as I write this; I figure that's about one-third of the way through my life (I'm nothing if not optimistic!). What will the next two-thirds look like? Staring out at the desert beyond the Strip, I know better than to try and predict. But what's my greatest hope?

I hope we all find out who we are and who we're meant to be. I hope we take action to become that person. I hope we connect deeply with each other – because that is the answer to the question: "How do I find out who I am and who I'm meant to be?"

We are at a critical juncture in our culture. As chatbots and AI scripts are becoming more mainstream in sales and marketing, it's tempting to let them do the heavy lifting. After all, they seem to have a way of putting words together that make us look smarter. And how about those pretty AI photos we are all posting of ourselves? Call me crazy, but I think your real face reflects what's in your heart. The ideal version of you is the human version of you, not the idealized version of you.

Let's allow this next generation of technology to manage the knowledge so that we can manage the wisdom. So that we can tend to the soul. So that we can continue with the most important work at hand – building genuine relationships, from the heart, one person at a time.

I can't. *We* can.

APPENDIX: TIMELINE OF EVENTS

1979	Moved from South Africa to the US
1985	First drink
1988	Came out
1990	Graduated high school
1990	Trained with an Olympic horse trainer
1991	Became a professional horse trainer
1992	Worked at Arby's
1993	Sold penny stocks
1994–1998	Worked at Charles Schwab
1998–2000	Worked at an internet startup
2000	Transitioned from alcohol to cocaine
2001	Transitioned from cocaine to meth
2001	Lost $1 million, got evicted from my condo
2002–2008	Dealing drugs, homeless, multiple arrests
2008	Rehab
2009	Became a licensed real estate agent
2014	Bought a house
2018	Bought a horse
2018–present	Compete in showjumping competitions
2019	Became a certified high-performance coach
2019	Got married
2023	Became a published author with *Top of Heart*

ENDNOTES

[1] M. Alper, M.R. Durose, and J. Markman, *2018 update on prisoner recidivism: A 9-year follow-up period (2005–2014)*, Bureau of Justice Statistics Special Report (2018).

[2] M.L. Brecht and D. Herbeck, "Time to relapse following treatment for methamphetamine use: A long-term perspective on patterns and predictors" in *Drug and Alcohol Dependence*, 139 (June), 18–25 (2014).

[3] While recognizing that many class addiction as a disease, I am using the term "disease" here metaphorically rather than literally.

[4] G. Bartzokis, M. Beckson, P.H. Lu, N. Edwards, P. Bridge, and J. Mintz, "Brain maturation may be arrested in chronic cocaine addicts" in *Biological Psychiatry*, 51 (8), 605–611 (2002).

[5] M. Bangia, G. Cruz, I. Huber, P. Landauer, and V. Sunku, *Sales automation: The key to boosting revenue and reducing costs*, McKinsey & Company (2020). Available from: www.mckinsey.com/capabilities/growth-marketing-and-sales/our-insights/sales-automation-the-key-to-boosting-revenue-and-reducing-costs

[6] National Association of REALTORS®, *2021 profile of home buyers and sellers* (2021). Available from: https://cdn.nar.realtor/

sites/default/files/documents/2021-highlights-from-the-profile-of-home-buyers-and-sellers-11-11-2021.pdf

[7] National Association of REALTORS®, *Highlights from the NAR member profile* (2022). Available from: www.nar.realtor/research-and-statistics/research-reports/highlights-from-the-nar-member-profile

[8] M.D. Lieberman, *Social: Why our brains are wired to connect* (2013), 4-5.

[9] Brené Brown, *The power of vulnerability*, YouTube (2011). Available from: www.youtube.com/watch?v=iCvmsMzlF7o

[10] Brené Brown, *The power of vulnerability*, YouTube (2011). Available from: www.youtube.com/watch?v=iCvmsMzlF7o

[11] S.M. Johnson, *Attachment theory in practice* (2019), 7.

[12] R.D. Putnam, *Bowling alone: The collapse and revival of American community* (2000), 19.

[13] G. Maté, *In the realm of hungry ghosts: Close encounters with addiction* (2010).

[14] S. Alexander Haslam, C. Haslam, T. Cruwys, J. Jetten, S.V. Bentley, P. Fong, and N.K. Steffens, "Social identity makes group-based social connection possible: Implications for loneliness and mental health" in *Current Opinion in Psychology*, 43 (February), 161–165 (2022), 161.

[15] A. Leung, C. Kier, T. Fung, L. Fung, and R. Sproule, "Searching for happiness: The importance of social capital" in *Journal of Happiness Studies*, 12, 443–462 (2011), 443.

[16] D. Coyle, *How showing vulnerability helps build a stronger team*, ideas.ted.com (2018). Available from: https://ideas.ted.com/how-showing-vulnerability-helps-build-a-stronger-team/

[17] C. Kingston, *Your impostor moment: Breaking through the barriers of self-doubt* (2022), 99.

18 Merton, R. K., "The Self-Fulfilling Prophecy" in *The Antioch Review*, 8 (2), 193–210 (1948). Available from: https://doi.org/10.2307/4609267

19 T.-Y. Kim, E.M. David, T. Chen, and Y. Liang, "Authenticity or self-enhancement? Effects of self-presentation and authentic leadership on trust and performance" in *Journal of Management*, 49 (3), 944–973 (2002).

20 C.G. Boeree, "Carl Rogers, 1902–1987" in *Personality theories* (1998, 2006). Available from: http://webspace.ship.edu/cgboer/rogers.html

21 D.H. Schunk, "Self-efficacy, motivation, and performance" in *Journal of Applied Sport Psychology*, 7 (2), 112–137 (1995).

22 R.Y. Kim, "What makes people happy? An empirical investigation of panel data" in *Applied Economics Letters*, 28 (2), 91–94 (2021), 91.

23 R. Mendius, *Train your brain #14: The power of intention* (2008), 3.

24 C. Rogers, *Client-centered therapy*, 3rd ed. (1956).

25 American Psychological Association, "Unconditional positive regard" in *APA dictionary of psychology* (2023). Available from: https://dictionary.apa.org/unconditional-positive-regard

26 A. Sadlier, "1 in 4 Americans feel they have no one to confide in" in *New York Post* (2019). Available from: https://nypost.com/2019/04/30/1-in-4-americans-feel-they-have-no-one-to-confide-in/

27 J. Suttie, "What you think about your emotions matters" in *Greater Good Magazine* (2019). Available from: https://greatergood.berkeley.edu/article/item/what_you_think_about_your_emotions_matters

28 B.Q. Ford, P. Lam, O.P. John, and I.B. Mauss, "The psychological health benefits of accepting negative emotions and thoughts: Laboratory, diary, and longitudinal evidence" in *Journal of Personality and Social Psychology*, 115 (6), 1075–1092 (2018).

[29] B.Q. Ford, J.O. Dmitrieva, D. Heller, Y. Chentsova-Dutton, I. Grossmann, M. Tamir, Y. Uchida, B. Koopmann-Holm, V.A. Floerke, M. Uhrig, T. Bokhan, and I.B. Mauss, "Culture shapes whether the pursuit of happiness predicts higher or lower well-being" in *Journal of Experimental Psychology: General*, 144 (6), 1053–1062 (2015).

ABOUT THE AUTHOR

G rant Muller is a Certified High Performance Coach™ and real estate agent on a mission to help high achievers who have tried every tool and tactic to sell more, achieve more, and find more fulfillment, but aren't quite making the progress they desire. Grant knows what it takes to sell, and sell well, and it all starts with a heart-centered approach. He volunteers on the board of One Colorado to ensure *all* of us have a seat at the table. When he's not coaching or working in real estate, you can find Grant competing with his horse and enjoying downtime with his husband and Pomeranians.

To contact Grant for speaking, coaching, and media inquiries, please visit http://www.grantmuller.com.

INDEX

Printed in the USA
CPSIA information can be obtained
at www.ICGtesting.com
JSHW021503180923
48673JS00002B/9